BOTTLE AND THE BADGE

A Cop's Journey from Addiction to Atonement

McCarthy Barnes Jr.

POSSE Publishing LLC

To the **Creator**, for the gifts of life, health, and strength.

To my mother, **Kim Frazier**, and my father, **McCarthy Barnes Sr.** (RIP), whose steadfast values have greatly influenced the person I am today.

To my beloved wife, **Selena Barnes**, and my daughters, **Mackayla Barnes** and **Shelena Walker**, whose love and support motivate me every day.

To my brothers, **James**, **Reginald**, and **Kevin**, and my sister, **Jannetta**, for their unwavering love and support that they have provided throughout my life.

To my mentor, **John Benton**, whose guidance, and inspiration keep me aligned with God's purpose.

To the dedicated members of the police departments I served with, whose unwavering commitment to our communities exemplifies honor, integrity, and selflessness.

And to my valued colleagues at **McKesson**, including **Antuane**, **Ulises, and many others**, whose faith in my abilities have been a continual source of encouragement.

I am profoundly grateful to each of you for being my guiding lights.

CONTENTS

1

SHADOWS OF THE BADGE

Introduction

Part I: Innocence Lost

Family and Community

I was born in the heart of Washington, D.C., in a neighborhood bustling with life yet shadowed by the struggles of urban living. Growing up, I often felt the sun struggle to penetrate the concrete jungle where towering buildings loomed over narrow streets, their chipped paint and graffiti telling stories of resilience and hardship. I'm the third oldest of five siblings, sandwiched between my older brother, Marcus, and my older sister, Tasha. My two younger brothers, Jamal and Amir, often followed me around, eager to emulate their big brother.

Our small apartment was a whirlwind of activity, filled with the sounds of laughter, playful bickering, and the occasional shout from my mother when things got too loud. Every Saturday morning, before the sun fully rose, I would wake up to the smell of coffee brewing in the kitchen. My mother, a talented hairstylist, had already begun her day, preparing for the long shifts that would take her away from home. "You're my little man," she would say, ruffling my hair and handing me the lawnmower.

"Don't forget the Johnsons' yard!" she'd remind me with a smile gracing her lips as she deftly tied her hair back into a bun. The mornings were hectic, but I loved the routine. It made me feel important.

Cutting grass wasn't just a chore; it was a chance for me to contribute and feel a sense of responsibility. As I pushed the mower across the neatly trimmed lawns of our neighbors, I would chat with them, soaking in their stories and laughter.

"Good job, David! You're becoming quite the landscaper!" Mr. Johnson would joke while patting me on the back. I beamed at the praise, my heart swelling with pride for my small contributions to the community. I loved the way the sun felt on my skin and the fresh smell of cut grass that lingered in the air.

Passions and Pastimes

After finishing the yard work, I would rush to the local boxing gym, where I had found my true passion. The moment I stepped inside, the smell of sweat and leather wrapped around me like a familiar embrace. The gym was alive with energy—fighters sparred in the ring, trainers shouted encouragement, and the rhythmic thud of gloves hitting heavy bags filled the air.

"Keep your guard up!" my coach would yell, and I would focus with determination lighting up my eyes. Boxing taught me discipline, resilience, and the importance of hard work. Every punch thrown felt like a step closer to becoming the man I aspired to be. I had started boxing at the age of eight, inspired by a local champion who often visited the gym to share his story.

One Saturday after a particularly grueling training session, I sat on the edge of the ring, panting and sipping water. An older boxer, seeing my exhaustion, approached me. "You've got heart, kid. Keep at it, and you'll go far," he said while clapping me on the shoulder. Those words echoed in my mind, fueling my ambition and reminding me that I was capable of greatness.

In the evenings, when I returned home, the kitchen would be filled with the sounds of my mother and grandmother preparing dinner. The rich aromas of simmering stews and fresh-baked bread swirled through the air. They would draw me in like a magnet. I often found myself lingering in the doorway, watching them work together, sharing stories, laughter, and recipes that had been passed down through generations.

"Come here, David! Help me with the greens," my grandmother would call, her hands moving deftly as she chopped vegetables. I rushed over, eager to learn her culinary secrets. As we cooked, she would share stories of our family's history and pass down wisdom with each slice of the knife.

"Cooking is like life, David. You have to season it just right, or it'll be bland," she would say with a wink. I would laugh, absorbing her lessons with a seriousness beyond my years. Those afternoons spent in the kitchen fostered a deep appreciation for family and tradition, and I learned to value the time spent with loved ones.

Childhood Dreams

My dreams extended beyond the boxing ring. I often daydreamed about becoming a police officer, inspired by the local officers who visited schools to promote safety and community. The sight of those uniforms filled me with a sense of pride and purpose. I envisioned myself as a guardian of justice; I wanted to be someone who would protect and serve my neighborhood.

After church every Sunday, I would linger in the community center, listening to the stories of officers who had made a difference. As they spoke of bravery and sacrifice, they ignited a fire within my heart. I imagined myself wearing a badge, bringing hope to those in need, just as the officers had done for me. The dream felt tangible, and I often practiced my lines in the mirror, imagining how I would address the community in times of need.

But my dreams were also shaped by the vibrant world around me. My mother's hairstyling business thrived in our community. She didn't just transform hair; she transformed lives. I would watch her work her magic; Her hands skillfully weaved through heads as she created stunning styles. The joy on her clients' faces filled me with admiration. I often thought about how my mother's work made people feel beautiful and confident, and I wanted to bring that same sense of pride to others.

Church and Community

Every Sunday, my family gathered for church. This tradition anchored us amidst the chaos of our lives. The community church, with its peeling paint and modest exterior, was a sanctuary for many families in the neighborhood. Inside, the air buzzed with warmth as familiar faces greeted us; Their smiles were a testament to the bonds we shared.

I loved the vibrant hymns that filled the sanctuary, the voices rising in unison, weaving a tapestry of hope and faith. I watched my mother's face light up during the choir's performances, her spirit lifting with each note. It was a reminder of the values we held dear—kindness, service, and the strength that came from faith.

After the service, I often found myself lingering, helping to clean up or volunteering for community events. The church was more than a place of worship; it was a hub of support and connection. I learned the importance of giving back, understanding that even small acts of kindness could create ripples of change in our community.

Fishing with Dad

Fishing was another cherished pastime. On warm Saturday mornings, I would accompany my father to the nearby river, where the water sparkled under the sun. With a rod in hand, I would sit quietly on the bank and listen to the gentle lapping of the waves and the chirping of birds. Those moments of tranquility were a welcomed escape from the bustling energy of our lives.

"Patience, son," my father would say, casting his line with practiced ease. "Fishing isn't just about catching fish; it's about enjoying the time spent together."

As we waited for a bite, we shared stories—my father recounting tales from his own childhood and me excitedly sharing my dreams of becoming a police officer. My father listened intently, nodding with pride. "You'll make a great officer one day. Just remember to always do what's right," he advised.

Those quiet moments by the river were some of my fondest memories. Here, surrounded by the beauty of nature and the comfort of family, I found clarity and purpose. I was not just a boy growing up in Washington, D.C.; I was a part of something larger, a legacy of strength and hope.

The Power of Dreams

As I navigated the complexities of childhood, I began to forge my identity. The boxing gym, church, family meals, and fishing trips all contributed to a rich tapestry of experiences that shaped my values. With each passing day, I felt the weight of my dreams grow heavier—dreams of becoming a police officer and serving my community.

But as I approached my teenage years, the innocence of childhood began to wane. The world outside my apartment was filled with challenges, and the allure of the streets started to creep in. I found myself at a crossroads; I was torn between the dreams instilled in me by my family and the temptations of a life I had once avoided.

When I laid in bed at night, I would often think about my future. I wondered if I would be able to hold on to the values my mother and grandmother had taught me? Would I be able to resist the distractions that beckoned from the streets? With determination in my heart, I vowed to stay true to myself, to honor the legacy of love and strength that surrounded me.

Little did I know that the choices I would soon face would test those values in ways I could never have imagined.

Part II: The Turning Point

The Shift

As I entered middle school, the innocence of childhood began to fade. The pressures of adolescence weighed heavily upon me. The allure of the streets grew stronger, and the friends I once played with began to drift toward the wrong crowd. Peer pressure became a formidable force, and I found myself torn between the path I wanted to follow and the one that laid before me.

Tasha, my older sister, had always been a guiding light in my life. She excelled in school and often encouraged me to stay focused on my dreams. "You can't let anyone pull you down," she would say. Her voice was stern, yet loving. But as she entered high school, she became more absorbed in her social life, and I felt the absence of her support.

Marcus, my older brother, had taken a different route. He used to be my role model but he started to hang with the wrong crowd. He spent more time on the streets than at home. I watched, with growing concern, as Marcus's choices began to spiral out of control. We had always shared a close bond, but now, I felt a growing distance between us. It felt as if he was slipping away into a world that I feared.

The Wrong Crowd

One fateful afternoon, I found myself wandering the streets after school. The familiar route to the boxing gym was replaced by a detour with new friends. They were older kids who seemed to embody the freedom I craved. They introduced me to graffiti, skateboarding, and a lifestyle that felt thrilling yet dangerous. The thrill of rebellion, tinged with the fear of disappointing my family, pulled me deeper into a world I had once avoided.

At first, it was just hanging out. I felt cool and accepted. But as weeks turned into months, the group began to engage in activities that made me uncomfortable—stealing, vandalism, and more. I often found myself standing at the crossroads of right and wrong while my childhood dreams were slowly fading into the background.

The turning point came one evening when my new friends dared me to tag a wall in a nearby alley. The thrill of the moment drowned out my better judgment. "Come on, David! Just do it! Show us what you've got!" they shouted as they were egging me on. With a racing heart, I picked up the spray paint while feeling a mixture of excitement and dread.

As the bright colors splashed across the wall, adrenaline surged through me, but the moment was short-lived. The sound of sirens pierced the air, and panic set in. The group scattered, but I froze. I was caught in the headlights of an approaching police car.

The Run-In with the Law

The officer who stepped out of the car was familiar. It was Officer Davis, the very same officer who had visited my school and inspired my dreams of becoming a police officer. My heart sank as I felt the weight of shame wash over me.

"David! What are you doing here?" Officer Davis's voice carried a blend of concern and disappointment. I stammered, trying to explain, but the words wouldn't come. I felt small and ashamed. The weight of my choices were crashing down on me.

"Get your friends and go home", Officer Davis said sternly. "You know better than this, David." My fear of him, sparked by the authority in his voice, was a stark contrast to the boyhood admiration I once felt for him.

As I walked home that night, the shame morphed into self-loathing. I had let myself down, and worse, I had disappointed the very people who looked up to me—my family, my community, and Officer Davis. That night, I laid in bed. I was staring at the ceiling and grappling with the reality of what I had done. The dreams of wearing a badge felt distant now because they were overshadowed by the weight of my actions.

Part III: A Path Divided

Reflection and Regret

After the incident, I retreated to myself while grappling with the aftermath. I faced ridicule from classmates and disappointment from my mother. The shame weighed heavily on me as I tried to navigate the complicated feelings of being a teenager torn between two worlds.

My siblings noticed the change in me. Tasha, always the protective sister, confronted me one evening while we were washing dishes. "What's going on with you?" she asked, with concern etched on her face. "You haven't been yourself lately."

I hesitated with the words caught in my throat. "I messed up, Tasha. I got caught tagging a wall. Officer Davis... he was there. He saw everything."

Her expression softened. "You're not your mistakes, Nigeria. You have to remember who you are. You're destined for bigger things."

Unfortunately, the echoes of Tasha's words faded as I sank deeper into a pit of despair. The images of that night haunted me; I struggled to reconcile the boy who wanted to protect his community with the teenager who had crossed the line.

Seeking Redemption

Determined to reclaim my life, I focused on school again, throwing myself into my studies and rediscovering my passion for boxing. I started volunteering at community centers and mentoring younger kids who looked up to me. I hoped to instill the same values my mother had taught me in them.

As I reconnected with the boxing gym, the familiar sounds of gloves hitting bags and the encouragement of my coach reignited a spark within me. "You're back, kid! Let's see what you've got," my coach said with a grin spreading across his face.

With each punch, I felt the weight of my shame lift slightly. Boxing became my sanctuary once more because it was a place where I could channel my anger and frustration into something positive. I poured my heart into training. I was driven by a newfound determination to prove myself.

Reconnecting with the Dream

As I approached my senior year, I began to envision a future where I could reclaim my childhood dreams. I enrolled in a criminal justice program at my high school with determination to learn everything I could about law enforcement. I sought inspiration from the officers in my community by attending neighborhood meetings and volunteering for ride-alongs when I could.

The more I learned, the more I realized the complexity of the badge I had once idolized. I met officers who were not just enforcers of the law but also advocates for change. They fought to bridge the gap between the police and the community. Their stories resonated with me and ignited a fire within my heart that had dimmed for far too long.

It was during this time that I made a pivotal decision: I chose to join the police department. I didn't only want to wear a badge, but I wanted to embody the principles of justice and service. I wanted to be the officer who inspired hope and showed kids like me that there was a way out of the darkness.

With a renewed determination, I prepared for the police academy as soon as I graduated high school. The journey was arduous and filled with physical and mental challenges, but I welcomed each hurdle as a test of my resolve. I forged bonds with fellow recruits. We shared stories of our pasts, and together, we envisioned a future where we could make a difference.

Part IV: Redemption

The Academy

As I donned the uniform for the first time, a wave of emotions washed over me. The weight of the badge felt heavy, but it was a weight I welcomed. I was no longer the boy in a Halloween costume; I was a man committed to serving and protecting my community.

Building Trust

As I became a respected officer, I forged connections with the community. I earned their trust and respect. I engaged in outreach programs and organized events to foster positive relationships between officers and residents. I became known for my approachable demeanor and genuine care for the people I served. I embodied the ideals I had cherished since childhood.

However, the weight of my past choices lingered. The shadows of that night in the alley, the disappointment in Officer Davis' eyes, and the burden of my mistakes were ever-present reminders of the fine line I walked.

2

THE BADGE WEIGHS HEAVY

The Week Before Graduation

I stood in front of the mirror and adjusted my uniform for what felt like the hundredth time. The crisp blue fabric hugged my form, and I took a moment to appreciate the significance of the badge pinned to my chest. In just a week, I would graduate from the police academy. I had dreamed of this moment for as long as I could remember. Now that it was here, a knot of anxiety tightened in my stomach.

Today was my first shift on the streets. This day would test everything I had learned. The weight of expectation pressed down on me like a heavy mist. Taking a deep breath, I reminded myself of why I chose this path.

Responding to a Horrific Traffic Accident

The day began like any other, but I could sense the weight of anticipation in the air. My partner for the day, Officer Reyes, was a veteran with years of experience. He had a reputation for being tough but fair, and I was eager to learn from him.

As we cruised through the city in our patrol car, the radio crackled to life. "Unit 12, respond to a 10-50 at the intersection of 14th and Constitution. Multiple injuries reported."

My heart raced as I glanced at Reyes. "Let's go!" I shouted, with adrenaline surging through my veins.

We arrived moments later, and the sight was gut-wrenching. Two cars had collided at high speed. One of them was a mangled wreck that looked like a crushed soda can. Sirens and shouting filled the air as emergency responders worked to free those trapped inside.

I jumped out of the car and ran toward the chaos. My training began to kick in as I quickly assessed the situation. A woman was screaming and clutching her knee, A man in the other vehicle was unconscious with blood seeping from a gash on his forehead. I knelt beside him, checking for a pulse. There was a weak but steady heart rate.

"Stay with me, sir!" I said. My voice was steady despite the panic rushing through my veins. "Help is on the way."

The woman continued to scream, and I turned to her. "What happened?", I asked.

"I—I don't know! We were just driving, and then—" she stammered with tears streaming down her face.

"Take a deep breath. Help is here. Just stay calm." I could feel the weight of the moment pressing down on me. I had trained for this, but nothing could prepare me for the raw impact of human suffering.

Once the paramedics took over, I stepped back to collect my thoughts. The chaos began to fade, but the images of the wreckage burned into my mind. I had trained for this, but the reality was far more visceral than I had anticipated.

The Aftermath

Later that day, as we finished our shift, Reyes and I sat in our patrol car. The weight of the morning's events were hanging in the air. "It never gets easier," he said to break the silence. "But you learn to cope."

"I thought I was ready," I confessed while running my hands through my hair. "But seeing it up close... it's different."

"Trust me, it's normal to feel overwhelmed. Just remember why you're here. You're making a difference, one call at a time." His words offered me some comfort, but the images of that accident still lingered in my mind.

As I laid in bed that night, I replayed every detail—the sounds, the sights, the emotions. I had chosen this path to protect and serve, but the weight of it was beginning to feel overwhelming.

Capturing a Robber

The next day, we were called to a local convenience store where a robbery was in progress. My heart raced as we sped through the city with flashing lights and sirens.

"Unit 12, respond to a robbery at the corner store on 5th Street," the dispatcher informed us.

As we arrived, I saw the store clerk visibly shaking while pointing toward the exit. "He ran that way!" she shouted with a trembling voice.

"Let's go!" Reyes instructed. I nodded with adrenaline surging once more. We dashed out of the store. Our boots were pounding against the pavement.

Without a second thought, I sprinted down the street and scanned for any sign of movement. The rush of the chase filled me with purpose. Then I spotted him—a man in a dark hoodie who clutched a purse as he turned the corner.

"Stop!" I yelled. My voice echoed through the alley. He glanced back with eyes wide and full of fear. Then, he took off running.

I chased after him with my legs burning. I was fueled by determination. "You can't escape!" I shouted as I pushed myself harder.

As I rounded the corner, I tackled him to the ground. The impact knocked the wind out of both of us. "Get off me!" he growled as he struggled against my grip.

"Not a chance," I replied. My voice was steady as I restrained him. Adrenaline coursing through me. I felt the thrill of the chase and the satisfaction of doing my job.

Once the cuffs were on, I stood up, panting. The elderly lady who had been robbed approached with tears of relief streaming down her face. "Thank you," she whispered. Her voice was choked with emotion. In that moment, I felt a rush of pride. Even though it was small, I had made a difference.

The Emotional Weight

As I walked back to the patrol car, the thrill began to fade. It was replaced by a weight I couldn't quite place. I had done my job, yet the echoes of the robbery replayed in my mind. I could still see the fear in the clerk's eyes and the relief of the elderly lady. The darkness of the streets felt suffocating.

That night, I sat on my bed and stared at the ceiling. I had chosen this path to protect and serve, but each encounter left a mark—a reminder of the fragility of life and the darkness that lurked beneath the surface.

The DUI Arrest

The following day, my shift took another turn. We were called to assist with a suspected DUI. As we arrived at the scene, I could see a car swerving erratically down the street and narrowly missing parked vehicles.

"Get ready," Reyes said with a serious tone. We pulled the patrol car, with flashing lights, behind the swerving vehicle.

I approached cautiously with my hand resting on my holster. "Driver, step out of the vehicle!" I commanded. I tried to maintain a calm demeanor despite the tension in the air.

A man stumbled out with bloodshot eyes. He was reeking of alcohol. "What's the problem, officer?", he slurred with a goofy grin plastered on his face.

"Do you even know where you are?", I replied with frustration bubbling beneath my surface.

After a series of failed sobriety tests, it became clear that he was too intoxicated to drive. I cuffed him and placed him in the back of the patrol car. My heart was heavy with the knowledge that this was just another day in the life of a police officer.

The Bar Culture

After each shift, it became part of the culture to unwind at a local bar with my colleagues. It was a ritual—a way to decompress and share the weight of our experiences. As I entered the dimly lit bar, the familiar sounds of laughter and clinking glasses greeted me.

"Hey, Nigeria! Over here!" Reyes called while waving me over to a booth filled with fellow officers.

As I joined them, I could feel the tension of the day begin to melt away. "Rough shift?" one of the officers asked while sliding a cold beer my way.

"You have no idea," I replied as I took a long sip. The cool liquid felt refreshing, but it also reminded me of the darker moments I had just faced.

A Night of Revelry

As the night wore on, the atmosphere grew lively. We shared stories, laughed at the absurdities of our jobs, and for a moment, the weight of our duties felt lighter. But as the clock ticked closer to midnight, tensions began to rise. A group at the bar started eyeing us suspiciously. Their glares eventually turned into whispered comments.

"Did you hear what they said?", one of my colleagues grumbled while clearly annoyed. "They think we're just a bunch of wannabes."

"Let's just ignore them," I suggested, but Reyes was already standing with clenched fists.

"Hey! You got a problem?" he shouted across the room with a rising voice.

Panic shot through me. "Reyes, sit down!" I urged, but it was too late. The other group stood up, and suddenly we were face to face.

"Yeah, we do! You think you're better than us?", one guy sneered as he stepped forward.

I could feel the tension crackling in the air, and I knew this could escalate quickly. I stepped in front of Reyes and tried to diffuse the situation. "Hey, we're just here to unwind. No need for this," I said with a calm, but stern voice.

As the words left my mouth, I felt a shove from behind. In an instant, chaos erupted. Drinks spilled, chairs toppled, and voices rose in anger. Reyes was pushing back against the other guy and I could see the situation spiraling out of control.

Stepping In

"Enough!", I shouted while stepping in between them. "We're all on the same side here. Let's not do this!" My heart raced as I tried to keep my colleagues from making a mistake that could have serious repercussions.

Finally, cooler heads prevailed. The tension eased slightly, and the other group backed off while muttering under their breath as they returned to their seats. I could see the anger in Reyes's eyes, but I knew we had dodged a bullet.

"Thanks for stepping in," Reyes said with a low voice as he sat back down. "I almost lost it there."

"Yeah, we can't afford to get into trouble like that," I replied while trying to shake off the adrenaline that was still coursing through me.

The Emotional Toll

As the night winded down, I couldn't shake the unsettling feeling that had settled in my gut. We had come so close to crossing a line that could have ended our careers. I had to focus on the job, but the shadows of my experiences loomed large.

That night, I laid in bed while staring at the ceiling. I had chosen this path to protect and serve, but the weight of the badge felt heavier each day. If I was going to keep my head above water, I had to find a way to cope with the emotional toll.

A New Challenge

The next week began with a call that would test my resolve even further. I was still riding the high of my recent arrests, but the weight of my early experiences hung over me. As I reported for duty, I could feel the familiar mix of anxiety and excitement.

"Unit 12, respond to a domestic disturbance at 123 Maple Street," the dispatcher announced. My stomach dropped because domestic calls were often unpredictable and could escalate quickly.

"Let's go," Reyes said, with a serious demeanor. We arrived at the scene, and I could already hear raised voices from inside the apartment.

As we approached the door, I took a deep breath while trying to mentally prepare myself for whatever laid ahead. Reyes knocked firmly. "Police! Open up!"

The door swung open, revealing a disheveled man and a woman with tears streaming down her face. "He won't leave me alone!", she cried with a shaky voice.

"Sir, step outside," Reyes ordered while maintaining a steady tone. The man hesitated, but with a gentle push from Reyes, he stepped onto the porch.

"What's going on here?" I asked as I tried to gauge the situation. The woman was visibly shaken, and I could sense the tension in the air.

"He's been drinking and won't stop!" she exclaimed while pointing at the man who was now glaring at her.

As we talked to both parties, I could feel the weight of the moment pressing down on me. I had been trained to handle situations like this, but seeing the fear in her eyes made my heart ache.

Making a Decision

After assessing the situation, it became clear that the man needed to be taken into custody. I could see the anger boiling in him, and I knew we had to act quickly. "I'm going to need you to step back, sir," I said firmly with my hand resting on my holster.

He lunged toward me, and instinct kicked in. In one swift motion, I grabbed him and brought him to the ground. "You're under arrest for domestic disturbance," I announced. I began cuffing him as he struggled.

The relief on the woman's face was palpable, and for a moment, I felt a surge of pride. I had made a difference again. However, as I led the man away, I couldn't shake the feeling that this was just *another* reminder of the darkness that existed in our city.

The Unforeseen Discovery

As I escorted the man to the car, something caught my eye—a glint of metal on the ground near the porch. I bent down and picked it up. I discovered a small silver locket. It was intricately designed and I could tell it had sentimental value.

"Hey, is this yours?" I asked the woman while holding it out for her to see.

Her eyes widened with tears of gratitude streaming down her face. "Yes! That belonged to my grandmother!"

In that moment, I felt a mixture of relief and joy. I had not only helped her in a difficult situation but also retrieved something precious to her. I tucked the locket into my pocket and promised to get it back to her after the situation settled.

However, as I drove away from the scene, the locket felt heavier than it should have. I had no idea how it had ended up in that front yard, and I couldn't shake the feeling that it might be tied to something deeper that I had yet to uncover.

After that call, I felt emotionally drained. Each shift seemed to pile on more weight than the last. I wondered if I was cut out for this. I had chosen this career to protect and serve, but the reality of it was beginning to feel overwhelming. I had faced challenges that tested my strength and resolve, but each encounter left me with a sense of unease. I had to remind myself that I was making a difference, even if it didn't always feel that way.

The Night of Reflection

That evening, I laid in bed while staring at the ceiling with the locket resting beside me. I thought about the woman's gratitude, but the weight of that nagging mystery loomed large. What if the locket held secrets? Was it connected to something I didn't yet understand?

As I drifted into sleep, my mind raced with possibilities. The badge I wore was not just a symbol of authority; it was also a reminder of the responsibility I had chosen to embrace. Each day brought new challenges and new mysteries. I had to stay sharp.

The Unfolding Mystery

The next day, I returned to work with the locket still weighing on my mind. I had decided to make it my mission to learn more about it. As I arrived at the station, I could feel the familiar mixture of anxiety and excitement.

"Hey, Nigeria! Ready for another day?", Reyes asked, with a grin on his face.

"Yeah, but I've got something on my mind," I replied while pulling the locket from my pocket. "Found this at a domestic disturbance last night. The woman said it belonged to her grandmother."

Reyes examined it closely. "It looks valuable. You should talk to her again. Maybe there's a story behind it."

I nodded and felt a surge of determination. "I think I will. It might lead to something important."

The Call

Later that day, we received a call about a suspicious person loitering near the same convenience store where I had captured the robber. My heart raced. This was my chance to dig deeper into the mystery of the locket.

"Unit 12, respond to a report of a suspicious person at the corner store on 5th Street," the dispatcher informed us.

"Let's go," I said with excitement bubbling up inside me.

When we arrived, I spotted the man—a scruffy figure with a weathered face who was pacing back and forth. I felt a strange pull to him. It felt as if he could have held clues to the past I was trying to unravel.

"Hey! You!", I called out as I approached him. "What are you doing here?"

He stopped and assessed us with narrowing eyes. "Just waiting for a friend," he said in a low tone.

"Do you have any ID?" Reyes asked as he stepped in beside me.

The man hesitated. I could sense something was off. "I don't need to show you anything," he muttered with a flicker of defiance in his eyes.

The Confrontation

As I took a step closer, my instincts kicked in. "Listen, it's just a routine check. We're here to keep the peace. If you're not doing anything wrong, there's nothing to worry about."

"Yeah? Well, I'm done talking," he snapped and turned to walk away.

"Hold it right there!" I shouted while moving to block his path. "You're not going anywhere until we sort this out."

The tension in the air thickened as he glared at me. I could feel my heart pounding in my chest and adrenaline surging as I prepared for a confrontation.

"Back off!" he shouted while shoving me aside.

In a flash, I grabbed his arm, twisted it behind his back, and forced him to the ground. "You're under arrest!" I announced, my voice steady despite the chaos unfolding around us.

As I cuffed him, I noticed something glinting in his pocket. I reached in and pulled out a small, familiar object—the other half of the locket I had found the night before.

The Connection

My heart raced as I held it up. "Where did you get this?" I demanded, my voice firm.

He looked up at me with surprise flashing across his face. "I—I don't know what you're talking about."

"This belongs to a woman I helped last night. You need to tell me what you know!" The weight of the moment pressed down on me, and I felt the pieces of the puzzle beginning to come together.

"I found it," he muttered, with a fading bravado. "I didn't mean to take it. I was just trying to survive."

"Trying to survive?" I echoed while my heart ached for the lives intertwined in this tangled web. "What does that even mean?"

The Revelation

As we transported him to the station, I pressed for answers. "You need to be honest with me. This is bigger than just a locket. What do you know about the woman?"

He hesitated, but finally spoke. "She was involved in something... something dangerous. I didn't mean to get caught up in it. I just needed money."

My mind raced as I connected the dots. The locket, the robbery, this man—there was a story here, a thread that tied everything together.

The Unfolding Mystery

Back at the station, I couldn't shake the feeling that I was on the brink of uncovering something significant. I needed to talk to the woman again. I had to dig deeper into her life and the secrets hidden within that locket.

As I prepared to follow up, I felt a mixture of excitement and fear. What if this led me to something dangerous? The streets were unpredictable, and I had seen the darkness they could harbor firsthand.

Despite this, I had made a promise to protect my community. I could not back down now.

As I settled into my desk, I could feel the weight of the badge pressing down on me. The challenges ahead were daunting, but I was ready to face them. One shift at a time, I would uncover the truth, no matter where it led.

3

AFTER THE SHOT

As I took my seat in the roll call room, a palpable tension hung in the air that was thick enough to cut with a knife. Officer Reyes sat beside me as he was flipping through reports of the recent surge in robberies and homicides. Each page turned felt like a countdown to a storm. The captain's voice echoed that this report was a grim reminder of the threats we faced every day. He emphasized the descriptions of possible suspects linked to recent homicides and robberies. It was a stark warning that our city was teetering on the edge of chaos.

"Keep your eyes peeled out there, folks," he said with a gaze sweeping across the room as he was trying to instill urgency. "We're counting on you to stay sharp. Lives depend on it."

Once roll call wrapped up, Reyes and I hit the streets. The weight of the morning's briefing pressed down on us like a heavy shroud. We decided to swing by the local corner store for a much-needed coffee and a brief respite from the chaos that was sure to come. The sun was just beginning to rise. Although it casted a golden hue over the city, I knew the beauty of the dawn would be short-lived.

As I entered the store, the familiar bell chimed above me, but I couldn't shake the feeling that something was off. The air felt charged, as if the world was holding its breath. I approached the counter. As I was about to pay, a figure caught my eye. A guy stood behind the dumpster outside. His body was tense as he was peering nervously around the corner. I couldn't shake the feeling that he was watching me, and my instincts screamed that something wasn't right.

I grabbed my coffee and rushed back to the patrol car where Reyes was waiting. "You won't believe what just happened," I said while sliding into the passenger seat with a racing heart and mind.

"I saw that!" Reyes replied. His brow was furrowing as he glanced in the rearview mirror. "What the hell was that guy doing?"

We decided to play it cool and eased out of the parking lot as if we were heading somewhere else. I kept my eyes glued to the rearview, and sure enough, the same guy stepped out from behind the dumpster. He glanced back at the store and his expression shifted from curiosity to panic. My heart pounded like a drum in my chest. I rifled through the clipboard of wanted suspects with adrenaline coursing through my veins. The descriptions matched a robbery from just a few days ago.

"Let's turn around," I said. My voice was steady but my insides were churning. "We need to check this out."

Just as we prepared to make the U-turn, everything changed. The suspect spun around, pulled out a gun, and fired directly at us. "Shots fired! Shots fired!" I shouted while instinctively ducking low in my seat. Adrenaline flooded my system like ice water.

"Take cover!" Reyes yelled with a sharp voice amidst the chaos. He was already reaching for the radio. "Dispatcher, send backup! We're under fire!"

The world narrowed as the sound of gunfire began ringing in my ears. Adrenaline surged through me. Time slowed. I could feel my heart racing and each beat was a reminder of the life-threatening situation we were in. Reyes and I exchanged a look: a silent agreement that we wouldn't let this guy escape.

"Let's go!" I commanded, and we took off after him. My every instinct yearned to catch this guy before he could hurt anyone else. The city blurred around us. The sounds of sirens and the shouts of bystanders merged into a chaotic symphony.

As we pursued him, he dashed toward a traffic light. An unsuspecting bystander, who was blissfully unaware of the danger, was waiting there. My stomach dropped as I watched the suspect point his gun at the civilian to get him out of the car. My instinct screamed at me to intervene and save that life.

"Stop right there!" I shouted in desperation. "Let him go!" Unfortunately, the suspect was too far gone. In a moment of panic, while trying to speed off, he collided head-on with another vehicle. The sickening sound of metal crunching filled the air, but he didn't stop; he was a cornered animal that was desperate to escape.

"Hands up!" I yelled with my gun drawn. Adrenaline coursed through my veins like fire. "Let me see your hands!" I echoed in the chaos, but it felt like a whisper against the storm.

In a split second, he turned back toward us with eyes filled of fear and fury. Time seemed to slow down as I processed his next move. He raised his weapon again and instinct took over. I squeezed the trigger.

The gunshot echoed like thunder against the backdrop of the street. The suspect collapsed in a crumpled heap.

It all happened in a whirlwind. I felt a rush of emotions crashing over me: relief, fear, and an overwhelming sense of responsibility. I could hardly breathe as I approached the scene with my heart pounding in my chest. Reyes was right beside me. Both of us were in shock as the gravity of the moment sunk in.

Sirens wailed in the distance as backup was finally approaching. As I surveyed the chaotic scene, I felt the weight of my actions settle heavily on my shoulders. I knew this wouldn't be the last time I'd wrestle with the choices made on these unforgiving streets. Would I be blamed? Would I lose everything for doing my job?

Later that day, we found ourselves in a small, sterile conference room, faced with the internal affairs team. The atmosphere was tense. The fluorescent lights glared down on the harsh judges. They peppered us with questions and predatory expressions.

"Officer Reyes, can you describe the events leading up to the shooting?" one investigator asked while leaning forward with pen poised above his notepad.

I took a deep breath. My heart was still racing from the earlier adrenaline. "We were responding to a suspicious individual. He was acting erratic, and when we attempted to confront him, he drew his weapon and fired at us."

"Did you have any other options at that moment?" another investigator pressed, his eyes narrowing, scrutinizing my every move.

I glanced at Reyes, who nodded slightly in a mixture of support and caution. "No. He was a threat to us and to civilians. We had to act."

The questions continued. Each one was a reminder of the gravity of what had happened. I could feel the weight of the suspect's life pressing down on me. I was haunted by the image of the young man whose dreams extinguished in an instant. Finally, the questioning wrapped up, but the tension lingered in my chest. As we stepped out of the building, Reyes turned to me with an expression of concern and camaraderie.

"You did what you had to do, man. Don't let them get in your head," he said, but I could see the worry etched on his face.

"Yeah, I know," I replied, but the unease still gnawed at me. "Still feels heavy, though."

That night, after a long shift and a draining day, I found myself at a small liquor store as I was trying to shake off the weight of the day. I wandered the aisles and spotted Reyes at the back, examining a shelf of bottles.

"Hey, Reyes!" I called out. Then, his face lighted up. "You wouldn't believe it. I'm buying my first bottle of liquor tonight! Just need something to take the edge off, you know?"

I chuckled. The sight of him holding up a cheap bottle of whiskey somehow eased the tension. "Good idea. We all need something after a day like today."

He picked up the bottle while grinning like a kid. "Here's to the job, right?"

"Yeah, to the job," I echoed, raising an imaginary glass in solidarity. However, the words felt hollow. It was an empty toast to a life that was slipping away.

As we walked out into the night, I couldn't shake the feeling that the events of the day would linger in my mind for a long time. The excitement of the chase, the fear of the gunfire, and the weight of a life taken would haunt me. For now, I had to take a moment to breathe, enjoy a drink with a friend, and remind myself that we were in this together.

Little did I know that this first bottle of liquor was the beginning of a terrible habit that would eventually almost consume my life.

The days turned into weeks, and the adrenaline of that fatal encounter faded into the background. It was replaced by the monotony of everyday patrols. However, the weight of the shooting still lingered, and the internal affairs investigation hung over me like a dark cloud. I found myself replaying the events in my mind repeatedly and questioning every choice I'd made.

Reyes and I continued our shifts, but the camaraderie we once shared felt strained. It was as if an invisible barrier had formed between us and neither of us knew how to breach it. The thrill of chasing down suspects had dulled, and I could sense Reyes grappling with his own demons. We both seemed to be fighting our battles alone, even when we were side by side.

Each night, I found myself reaching for that bottle. The whiskey was becoming a crutch I leaned on more and more. At first, it felt like a reward—a way to unwind after a long shift. But as the days turned into nights filled with liquor, the warmth of the alcohol began to morph into a heavy blanket of numbness that was suffocating me.

I would sit on my couch, staring at the walls of my small apartment. The city's chaos faded into the background as I poured another drink. The initial thrill of being a cop and making a difference had been replaced by a haunting emptiness. The weight of the gunshot echoed in my mind and the face of the suspect continually flashed before me. I couldn't escape the feeling that I hadn't just taken a life—I'd taken a part of myself in the process.

Reyes would occasionally check in on me, but I could see the concern etched on his face. "You okay, man?" he'd ask with worry. Each time, I'd shrug it off and insist that I was fine. But deep down, I knew I was spiraling into darkness.

One night, after a particularly tough shift, I found myself sharing a drink with Reyes again. He had a bottle of whiskey in hand, but this time, he looked more serious. "You know, we can talk about this stuff," he said, pouring himself a glass. "You don't have to do it alone."

I looked at him with the weight of his concern heavy on my heart. "I appreciate it, but I'm fine," I lied as I whispered. The truth was, I was anything but fine. The alcohol had begun to take control. It was pulling me deeper into a cycle of numbness that felt impossible to escape.

As the months went by, the alcohol became more than a coping mechanism; it became my lifeline. I would wake up each morning with a pounding headache. The remnants of the night before clung to me like a shadow. I started to lose track of time, My shifts began to blur into a haze of whiskey and regret.

I began to isolate myself from friends and family. The once vibrant bond I had with Reyes faded into occasional text messages and brief conversations. I could sense his frustration growing, but the distance felt like a necessary barrier to protect him from my crumbling world.

One fateful evening, the weight of it all came crashing down. I sat alone in my apartment with a bottle of whiskey that was nearly empty. I was swirling its contents and experiencing turmoil in my mind. As I stared at the wall, the shadows lengthened and morphed into grotesque shapes that mirrored my inner chaos. The memories of that dreadful day: the gunfire, the chaos, and the life I took played like a broken record. Each repetition dug deeper into my conscience.

Suddenly, the weight of guilt became unbearable. I felt like I was drowning. I was gasping for air in a sea of despair. Tears streamed down my face. They were hot and uncontrollable. The suspect, a young man with dreams and hopes, was now reduced to a statistic. I imagined his family and the pain etched into their faces. This shattered something deep within me.

I grabbed my phone. My fingers trembled as I scrolled through my contacts. Reyes. I hesitated. I had the urge to reach out but I was battling the shame that held me hostage. The need to connect and to seek help overwhelmed me. I dialed.

"Reyes," I choked out when he answered. My voice was raw while breaking under the weight of my emotions. "I... I can't do this anymore."

"Where are you?" he asked. You could hear the concern in his voice.

"I'm at home," I said. I managed to get the words out. "I need you."

Within minutes, there was a knock at my door, and I stumbled to answer it. My heart was racing. Reyes stood there with worry etched on his face. His eyes scanned me to assess the damage. Without a word, he stepped inside. I collapsed onto the couch and buried my face in my hands.

"What happened?" he asked softly as he took a seat beside me.

"I thought I could handle it: the job, the shooting, and family problems" I confessed with a voice of thick emotion. "But every day feels like I'm just... falling. I've lost myself, Reyes. I don't know how to come back."

He sat quietly for a moment and allowed me to unravel. "You're not alone in this, you know. We all have our battles," he said. "You've got to talk about it. Let it out. You can't drown in this."

I looked at him with tears. Each drop was a release of the pain I had been holding inside. "I'm scared. Scared that I'll never be okay again. That I'll always feel this... this weight."

Reyes nodded. "It's okay to be scared. It's okay to feel lost. But you have to let someone in. You have to let me help you."

In that moment, I realized how much I had pushed him away. I had been running away from the very support I desperately needed. I took a deep breath. I felt the walls of isolation start to crack. "I don't want to fight this alone anymore," I said with my voice trembling.

Reyes reached out and placed a hand on my shoulder. "Then don't. We'll figure this out together. One step at a time."

The warmth of his words wrapped around me like a lifeline. For the first time in months, I felt a flicker of hope. As I leaned into his support, I knew the road ahead would be long and difficult, but I was ready to face it, no longer alone in the darkness. The journey to reclaiming my life had begun.

4

THE MENTAL BREAKDOWN

The days bled into one another. Each shift was more taxing than the last. The adrenaline that once fueled me became a heavy blanket of anxiety that was suffocating and relentless. Every siren, every shout, and every flash of blue lights made my heart race. It was a reminder of the chaos that lurked just beneath the surface of our city. I felt like I was walking a tight rope and teetering between duty and despair.

It wasn't just the shooting that haunted me. It was the accumulation of every traumatic moment I experienced on the job: the blood, the faces of victims, and the desperation in their eyes. I could still hear the cries of those I couldn't save; their voices echoed in my mind like a broken record. Each call and response felt like another brick added to an already crumbling wall.

I found myself avoiding conversations with my colleagues and retreating into the solitude of my thoughts. I used to relish the camaraderie and the shared stories over coffee, but now those moments felt like reminders of what I was losing. Reyes noticed my withdrawal.

His concerned glances were becoming more frequent, but I brushed him off and insisted I was fine. I wasn't fine. I was unraveling.

The tipping point came one evening when I was called to a domestic disturbance. As I entered the cramped apartment, the air was thick with tension. I was met with a scene that would replay in my nightmares. A mother cradled her child with tears streaming down her face, while a man stood over them with rage radiating from his every pore. I felt the familiar rush of adrenaline, but this time, it wasn't excitement; it was pure, unadulterated fear.

In that moment, everything crashed down around me. The sound of the child's cries broke through my defenses. At that moment, I was transported back to the shooting. The weight of my responsibilities felt unbearable. My heart raced as I struggled to maintain control. I felt the walls closing in. I managed to diffuse the situation, but as I walked back to the patrol car, I started shaking. The world around me blurred and I felt a wave of dizziness wash over me.

That night, I sat on my bed and stared at the ceiling. My thoughts spiraled into a dark abyss. I reached for the whiskey again with a hope to drown out the noise in my head. Unfortunately, the alcohol only heightened my anxiety and amplified the chaos within. I felt trapped in a cycle of despair. It became clear that I couldn't handle it alone anymore.

The next morning, I made the call. I'd been hesitant to seek help because I feared the stigmas that came with it. However, the weight of my experiences had become too much to bear. I scheduled an appointment with a psychologist. My heart pounded as I dialed the number. I was terrified of what I might uncover, but I knew I needed to confront the demons that had taken residence in my mind.

Walking into the psychologist's office felt like stepping into a foreign world. The sterile environment, the calm colors, and the soft lighting felt overwhelming. I sat in the chair with clammy palms as I waited for Dr. Harris to arrive. When she walked in, her warm smile immediately put me at ease, but I still felt the tension coiled in my chest.

"Thank you for coming in today, Officer Nigeria," she said gently with a soothing voice. "I know it can be difficult to talk about what you've been through."

I took a deep breath as the weight of my experiences flooded back. "I don't even know where to start," I admitted in a whisper.

"We can start wherever you feel comfortable," she replied with an open and inviting demeanor.

As the session unfolded, I found myself recounting the events that troubled me: the shooting, the domestic disturbance, and the relentless barrage of trauma that seemed to come with the territory of being a police officer. I talked about the guilt, the fear, and the overwhelming sense of helplessness that had seeped into every aspect of my life.

Dr. Harris listened intently. She nodded as I spoke and her empathy was palpable. "It's important to acknowledge that you're current feelings are a normal response to the experiences you've had," she said. "Many officers go through similar struggles. You're not alone in this."

Her words resonated with me, and for the first time in months, I felt a flicker of hope. We began to explore coping mechanisms:—breathing exercises, mindfulness techniques, and ways to process my emotions without turning to alcohol. I realized that I had been trying to suppress my feelings. I thought I could handle it all on my own. The truth was, I needed help and that was okay.

As the weeks went by, I continued to see Dr. Harris regularly. Each session was a step toward healing and a chance to unpack the heavy load I had been carrying. I learned to confront my past instead of running from it. I began to understand that seeking help didn't make me weak; it made me stronger.

Gradually, I started to reclaim pieces of myself that I thought I'd lost forever. The nightmares still lingered and the memories were painful. However, I was learning how to manage them. I started reaching out to Reyes again by sharing my struggles and allowing him to support me. The invisible barrier between us began to dissolve and I found solace in our renewed camaraderie.

Reyes called frequently to check in on me. One afternoon, he showed up unannounced with a gym bag slung over his shoulder. "Get ready, we're hitting the gym," he said with his usual bravado intact.

I hesitated because the thought of physical exertion felt daunting. "I don't know, man. I'm not really up for it."

He raised an eyebrow with a smile playing on his lips. "You need this. Trust me. It's time to sweat out some of that stress."

With a reluctant sigh, I grabbed my own gym clothes and followed him. The moment we stepped into the gym, the smell of sweat and determination enveloped me. Reyes led the way by pushing me to lift weights and run on the treadmill. Each drop of sweat felt like a release and a way to let go of the pent-up anxiety that clung to me.

After a grueling workout, I collapsed onto the bench while panting heavily. Reyes joined me with a broad grin on his face. "See? That wasn't so bad, was it?"

I chuckled while wiping the sweat from my forehead. "Okay, you were right. I needed that."

"Glad to hear it," he said, clapping me on the shoulder. "We'll make this a regular thing. It's as good for your mind as it is for your body."

As the days turned into weeks, I found solace in our gym sessions. The physical exertion began to clear my mind and I started to feel a sense of control returning. The endorphins worked wonders. They lifted my spirits and allowed me to process my feelings more clearly.

However, the emotional roller coaster was far from over. One evening, after a particularly exhausting day, I found myself spiraling again. I stared blankly at the wall as I was overwhelmed by the weight of my thoughts. The nightmares had returned, and despite my progress, I felt like I had taken two steps back for every step forward.

Desperate for connection, I decided to attend a local church service that Reyes had mentioned. "It's a great place to clear your head," he'd said. "You might find some peace there."

That Sunday, I walked into the modest church. The scent of polished wood and candle wax filled the air. The congregation was small, but the warmth enveloped me. I sat in the back and listened to the sermon. I allowed the words to wash over me. The pastor spoke about healing, resilience, and the importance of community.

Tears prickled at the corners of my eyes as I realized how isolated I had felt. I had been so focused on my struggles that I had forgotten the strength that comes from sharing our burdens. When the service ended, I felt uplifted. A glimmer of hope ignited within me.

Afterward, I approached the pastor and shared a bit of my story. He listened intently, offered words of encouragement, and reminded me that it was okay to seek support. "You're not alone, Officer. There's strength in vulnerability," he said while placing a hand on my shoulder.

That moment of connection stayed with me as I left the church. My heart felt a little lighter. I realized I needed to reach out more and let others in. I began attending POSSE meetings (Police Officer Sobriety Support Enbloc). This was a gathering of officers who share their experiences and support one another. It was a safe space that was free from judgment. I could be open about my struggles.

At the meetings, I heard stories that mirrored my own: officers grappling with trauma, guilt, and the pressures of the job. Each shared experience resonated deeply and I felt a sense of camaraderie that I hadn't felt in a long time. It was refreshing to know I wasn't alone in this fight.

Reyes continued to check in on me by visiting often. One evening, while sharing a couple of beers on my balcony, he looked me square in the eye. "I'm proud of you, man. You're doing the hard work. Just remember, it's okay to have tough days. You're human."

I nodded as the weight of his support grounded me. "Thanks, Reyes. I really appreciate you being here."

"Always," he replied while raising his bottle in a toast. "To progress, man. One day at a time."

As the week of my return to the streets approached, the emotional roller coaster reached its peak. I felt a mixture of excitement and dread. The two battled for dominance. Some days, I felt ready to don my uniform again and face whatever challenges that had lain ahead. Other days, I felt the fear surging back and whispering that I wasn't strong enough.

I spent that final week in a whirlwind of emotions. I focused on my therapy sessions, gym workouts, and church visits, all while grappling with the reality of returning to a job that had once been my passion. On one particularly trying day, I found myself lying on my bed and staring at the ceiling with tears streaming down my face. I felt lost and overwhelmed. The weight of my experiences pressed down on me like a ton of bricks.

In that moment of despair, I reached for my phone and called Reyes. He answered almost immediately and sensed my distress. "Hey, what's going on?"

"I'm scared, Reyes. What if I can't do this? What if I freeze up again?"

"Listen," he said firmly. "You've faced your demons. You've fought hard to get to this point. You're not the same officer you were before. You've grown. Just take it one call at a time. Trust yourself."

His words resonated deep within me and ignited a flicker of resilience. "You really think I can do this?"

"I know you can," he replied. "You have a community behind you now. You're not alone."

As we hung up, a wave of determination washed over me. I realized that, while the journey ahead would be challenging, I was no longer alone in this fight; I had the support of my friends, my colleagues, and the community around me.

5

FACING THE STREETS AGAIN

I attended a therapy session before returning to duty, and Dr. Harris encouraged me to focus on the progress I'd made.

"You've built a toolbox of strategies to help manage your feelings," she reminded me. "Trust that you can rely on them when the going gets tough."

I nodded, but doubt still crept in. "What if I can't handle the pressure?"

"Remember, it's okay to feel overwhelmed. Just take a moment, breathe, and reach out for support when you need it," she advised. "You are not alone in this."

Her words echoed in my mind as I returned home. I decided to hit the gym to clear my head. The workout felt cathartic. Each rep was a release of the tension that had built up over the week. As I finished, I caught a glimpse of my reflection in the mirror—sweaty, tired, but somehow stronger.

That night, I settled into bed, my thoughts raced with both excite-ment and fear about my return. I reached for my phone and texted Reyes: "Thanks for being there, man. I really appreciate it."

He replied almost instantly: "Always here for you. You got this!"

As the weekend approached, I made my way to church again. I was seeking the comfort of the community that had begun to feel like a second home. The pastor's words about hope and healing resonated deeply. I found myself tearing up as he spoke about the strength found in vulnerability.

After the service, I chatted with a few members of the congregation by sharing my journey and listening to their stories of resilience. Each conversation further solidified my belief that I was not alone; we all carried burdens and sharing them made them lighter.

That evening, Reyes came over for dinner. We cooked together while laughing and joking in the process. In those moments, I felt a sense of normalcy returning: a reminder that life could still be joyful despite experiencing challenges.

As we sat down to eat, I expressed my gratitude. "I don't think I could have gotten this far without you, Reyes. You've been my rock."

He waved a hand dismissively. "You did the hard work, man. I just helped you see it through."

With each passing day, I felt a growing sense of readiness. I pre-pared my uniform and ensured that everything was in order. The night before my return, I lied in bed while my stomach was a knot of nerves. I closed my eyes, focused on my breathing, and recited the affirmations Dr. Harris had taught me. "I am strong. I am capable. I am not alone."

Finally, the day arrived. I stood in front of the mirror in my crisp and clean uniform. I felt a mixture of excitement and trepidation swirling within me. As I drove to the precinct, my heart raced. The familiar streets felt different this time—charged with potential and uncertainty.

Upon arriving, I was greeted by the sounds of laughter and chatter and I was hit by a wave of nostalgia. As I walked through the doors, I felt the camaraderie of my fellow officers surrounding me and providing a comforting backdrop to the nerves that fluttered in my stomach.

The roll call began. As I took my seat, I was acutely aware of the collective energy in the room. The captain began the briefing and discussed the day's priorities. My mind was racing with thoughts of what had laid ahead. Would I be able to respond effectively? Would I be able to face the chaos without being overwhelmed?

After the briefing, Reyes walked over with an encouraging expression. "You ready for this?"

I took a deep breath. "As ready as I'll ever be."

He clapped me on the back. "Let's do it together. Just one call at a time."

With that, we stepped out into the bright morning light, and I felt a rush of determination. The streets awaited as they were filled with uncertainty and promise. I had spent weeks preparing for this moment. As I donned my badge, I felt a sense of purpose returning.

The first call came in shortly after we hit the streets: an altercation at a local bar. My heart raced as we arrived on the scene with the familiar sounds of chaos enveloping us. I felt the adrenaline kick in, and for a moment, it felt exhilarating.

As we approached the scene, I could hear raised voices and shouts. I took a deep breath and grounded myself in the techniques I had learned. I focused on the situation and reminded myself to stay calm and collected. Reyes and I moved in to assess the situation as we separated the individuals involved.

I was surprised by how quickly my training kicked in. I found my footing and managed to diffuse the situation without incident. As we walked away, I felt a rush of pride—a small victory in a long battle.

Over the next few days, I faced a variety of calls that each involved a new challenge. Some were daunting, while others were more routine. Each time, I relied on the tools I had developed to naviagate the emotional turbulence with newfound clarity.

Reyes stayed close and offered support and encouragement. After a particularly stressful shift, we sat down for coffee. "How are you feeling?" he asked while his brow furrowed with concern.

"Honestly? It's a mixed bag," I admitted. "Some moments feel amazing as I'm back in my groove. Other moments... it's still hard."

"That's normal," he said, nodding. "You're still processing every-thing. Just remember, it's a journey. You're doing great."

His words resonated with me and solidified the understanding that healing was not linear. Although I had faced my demons, I was still learning how to navigate the complexities of my emotions. It was okay to have tough days.

As the week progressed, I went through a whirlwind of emotions. Some moments felt invigorating; they filled with hope and determi-nation. Other moments plunged me into anxiety and doubt. How-ever, with each passing day, I felt stronger and more in control.

The final call of that week came in late on a Friday evening. It was a high-stakes situation—an armed robbery in progress at a convenience store. My heart raced, but I felt the familiar adrenaline surge. As we arrived on the scene, I took a moment to ground myself and recall all the techniques I had learned in therapy.

The chaos was palpable. Customers were screaming and the suspect was waving a gun around while demanding cash. I exchanged a glance with Reyes, who nodded with a calm and focused expression. We moved into position. We were ready to act.

In that moment, everything slowed down. I felt a sense of clarity wash over me. I was prepared for this. As I kept my eyes on the suspect, I reached for my radio and issued commands to the dispatcher for backup.

"Drop the weapon!" I shouted. "We can resolve this peacefully. Just put the gun down."

The suspect hesitated while his eyes darted between us and the frightened customers. I could feel the tension in the air, but I remained grounded and focused on de-escalating the situation. I could see Reyes moving in from the side. That was a calculated maneuver to flank the suspect.

"Let's talk," I continued in a calm voice. "No one needs to get hurt today."

To my surprise, the suspect lowered his weapon slightly with uncertainty flickering in his eyes. "I just need the money... I didn't want to hurt anyone!"

In that moment, I seized my chance. "We can help you. Just let us do that—put the gun down."

After a tense moment that felt like an eternity, the suspect finally dropped the weapon and surrendered to us. Relief washed over me as we moved in to secure him. The weight of the situation dissipated.

As we led him away, I felt a rush of emotion: a combination of adrenaline, relief, and pride. I had faced one of my biggest fears and proved I was stronger than it. Reyes clapped me on the back with a knowing smile on his face. "You did it, man. You really did it!"

That night, I laid in bed and stared at the ceiling. My heart was still racing from the events of the day. I felt a profound sense of accomplishment. I was back, not just as an officer, but as a person reclaiming my life.

The next day, I received a call from Dr. Harris to check in on my progress. I shared the details of the previous day's events as my voice brimmed with excitement. "I can't believe it, Doc. I faced my fear, and I didn't crumble."

"That's incredible, Officer Nigeria. You should be proud of yourself," she said, with a warm and encouraging voice. "Remember, this is just the beginning. Continue to build on your successes."

As I hung up the phone, I felt a renewed sense of hope. I knew that the road ahead wouldn't always be easy, but I was ready to face it. I was armed with the support of my community and the tools I had developed. I was no longer just surviving; I was thriving.

As the weeks turned into months, I continued to embrace the support of Reyes, the gym, church, and the POSSE meetings. Each element played a vital role in my journey toward healing. I learned that vulnerability was not a weakness but a strength. It was a powerful tool that allowed me to connect with others and find solace in shared experiences.

With each passing day, I felt more in control of my life. While the scars of my past would always remain, they no longer defined me. I was ready to face whatever may come next; one step at a time. I, Officer Nigeria, am a survivor.

6

NEW BEGINNINGS

The weeks rolled on in a blur. Each day in Unit 12 forged my resolve and resilience like steel in a fire. Just as I was beginning to find my footing again, a new rhythm emerged in my life—one I hadn't anticipated but welcomed with open arms.

My partnership with Reyes had reignited a camaraderie I thought I'd lost. Beyond the precinct, a different connection was blossoming. This one was both intoxicating and terrifying. Dr. Harris had become an essential part of my journey; her presence was a beacon in the tumultuous waters I navigated. Each session was a dance of emotions, and with every encounter, my feelings for her intensified. This revealed layers that I did not expect to confront.

One fateful afternoon, as we wrapped up our session, I lingered as if a magnetic pull urged me to stay. We had begun discussing coping strategies. Then, the conversation took a surprising turn. Dr. Harris shared a story about her love for painting; it was a passion that brought her solace amid chaos.

"I've always admired how creative you are, Dr. Harris," I said while leaning back in my chair. My voice remained steady despite the storm brewing inside me. "I can't imagine what it's like to express feelings through art."

"It's liberating," she replied as her eyes ignited with passion. "Art allows me to communicate emotions that words sometimes fail to capture."

As she spoke, I felt an undeniable connection. A current surged between us. There was something captivating about her presence and the way her words danced through the air. She ignited my imagination. The connection filled the room with an unspoken tension that both thrilled and terrified me.

"Maybe one day, you could show me some of your paintings," I suggested as courage flickered within me like a flame. The prospect was exhilarating. It felt like I was standing on the edge of a cliff; I was ready to leap into the unknown.

Dr. Harris smiled with a hint of mischief sparkling in her eyes. "I'd love that. Only if you promise to bring some of your infamous homemade cookies. Deal?"

"Deal," I replied as my heart raced at the thought of spending more time with her outside of the office.

The anticipation of our next meeting hung in the air like an electric charge. Each session felt infused with unspoken possibilities. I found myself daydreaming about her: her laughter, the way her hair fell softly over her shoulder, and how her eyes sparkled when she spoke about her passions.

One evening, after an especially enlightening session, I walked out of the office feeling lighter than air. However, before I could leave, Dr. Harris called out to me.

"Officer Nigeria, wait!" she said as her tone bursted with excitement. "I'm hosting a small gathering this weekend—just a few friends, some good food, and maybe a little music. I'd love for you to come."

My heart raced like a runaway train. "I'd really like that. Thank you for the invitation."

As we exchanged details, a flutter of anticipation twisted in my stomach. This wasn't just a professional relationship anymore; it was evolving into something deeper. This is what I had been yearning for.

On the night of the gathering, I stood before my mirror and adjusted my shirt for what felt like the thousandth time. I chose a fitted navy shirt, that showcased my physique, and paired it with dark jeans. I wanted to make a good impression, but more than that, I wanted to enjoy the evening without the shadows of my past looming over me.

When I finally arrived at Dr. Harris's apartment, the sounds of laughter and music engulfed me at the door. She opened it with her radiant smile lighting up the space. Her hair was cascading in soft waves and she was dressed in a simple, yet elegant, dress that accentuated her natural beauty.

"Hey, you made it!" she exclaimed as her eyes brightened. "I'm so glad you're here."

As I stepped inside, the warm ambiance enveloped me: soft lighting, the enticing aroma of home-cooked food, and a small group of friends mingling comfortably. A mixture of nerves and excitement coursed through me as I took in the scene.

"Let me introduce you to everyone," Dr. Harris said while guiding me through the crowd. She introduced me to her friends, who welcomed me with friendly smiles and easy conversation.

As the night wore on, I became increasingly aware of Dr. Harris's presence. We laughed together and I noticed the way her eyes sparkled when she spoke about her passions. Each shared glance felt electric and ignited a warmth I hadn't felt in a long time.

At one point, we found ourselves in the kitchen as we prepared snacks together. The playful banter flowed effortlessly as we chopped vegetables and shared stories. I felt a sense of ease in her presence, as the weight of my past slipped away like water off a duck's back.

"Can I ask you something?" I said while glancing at her as I handed her a bowl of hummus.

"Of course," she replied while looking up with curiosity.

"What made you choose this path? Therapy, helping people like us?" I gestured lightly. I wanted to understand the woman who had guided me through my darkness.

Dr. Harris paused. "I've always believed in the power of connection and healing. I want to help people find their way through the shadows. It's rewarding to see someone reclaim their life."

Her sincerity resonated deeply with me. "You're making a difference, you know. You've certainly made a difference in my life."

Just then, the atmosphere shifted. A sudden loud crash came from the living room and laughter halted. My instincts kicked in and I turned toward the sound with adrenaline spiking through me. I exchanged a glance with Dr. Harris as the tension in the room thickened.

"Stay here," I said. I moved toward the source of the noise as my training kicked in. As I stepped into the living room, I saw one of the guests had knocked over a lamp. It shattered on the floor.

"Just a little clumsy!" the guest said with a nervous laugh, but I could see the unease ripple through the crowd.

"Everyone okay?" I asked while scanning the room.

"Yeah, we're fine!" Dr. Harris called from behind me.

As I turned back to her, I felt a rush of protectiveness. "I think I'll help clean that up," I said while moving toward the scattered glass.

While we cleaned, the tension slowly dissipated and laughter returned to the room. However, I couldn't shake the adrenaline coursing through me. The unexpected moment reminded me how life was unpredictable. There was always sudden changes occurring.

When Dr. Harris's friends left for the night, she invited me to stay back, come to the balcony of her apartment, and look at the stars. As we stood on the balcony and gazed out at the city lights that twinkled like stars, I felt the pulse of the evening settle around us. The earlier chaos had faded. It was replaced by a comfortable silence that felt rich and meaningful.

"Thanks for inviting me tonight," I said while leaning against the railing. "I didn't expect to feel so at home."

"I'm glad you came. It's nice to see you outside of our sessions," she replied. Her voice was so soft against the night air.

In that moment, I felt a surge of courage. "I've enjoyed spending time with you, Dr. Harris. I mean, can I call you that still? Or should I just stick with 'Doctor'?" I teased as a smile tugged at my lips.

"Call me whatever you'd like," she replied with a hint of playfulness dancing in her tone. "But I think 'Hannah' might work just fine."

"Hannah," I repeated while savoring the name. "You can call me David. I'd like to get to know you better. Maybe over dinner sometime?"

Her eyes sparkled with delight. "I'd like that too, David."

As the city lights twinkled in the background, we shared a moment of silence. The air was charged with unspoken possibilities. Suddenly, a loud bang echoed in the distance and jolted us from our reverie. My instincts flared again and reminded me of the unpredictability that loomed outside our bubble of connection.

"Did you hear that?" I asked as concern tightened my chest.

Hannah nodded as her expression shifting. "It sounded like a gunshot."

My heart raced and the weight of my past crashed back down like a wave. "Stay here," I instructed, but she stepped closer with determination in her eyes.

"I'm coming with you," she insisted.

I hesitated. I was torn between my protective instincts and the need to keep her safe. "It might be dangerous."

"I can handle myself, David. You know that," she replied as her voice remained steady, but I could see the fear lurking behind her resolve.

With a deep breath, I nodded. "Alright, but stay close."

As we moved toward the source of the noise, adrenaline surged through me. The connection we had built felt fragile against the looming threat. However, I was determined to protect her. Together, we stepped into the unknown. We were ready to face whatever awaited us.

The night was far from over.

The moment we stepped outside, the atmosphere shifted. The distant sounds of laughter and music faded into an unsettling silence. They were replaced by the pulse of the city night that was tinged with tension. My senses heightened as I scanned the streets to search for any sign of danger. Hannah stood beside me. Her presence was both grounding and alarming.

"Stick close," I murmured in a low whisper. She nodded as her grip on my arm tightened. As we moved cautiously down a dimly lit alleyway, I felt the weight of her determination beside me. It was a force that both comforted and worried me.

The sounds of the city were muted but the echoes of the gunshot rattled in my mind. It had come from a few blocks away. This was a place where life had been vibrant just moments before. Now, it felt like a ghost town and the air was thick with anticipation.

"Do you think we should call someone?" Hannah asked. Although her voice was steady, I could sense the underlying anxiety.

"Yeah, but let's not draw attention to ourselves," I replied as my instincts kicked in. "We need to assess the situation first."

The streetlights casted eerie shadows. The city felt different at night; It was a living entity filled with secrets. A few people lingered on the corners. Their faces were illuminated by the glow of their phones. They were oblivious to the potential danger.

As we approached the corner, I noticed a group gathered near a storefront. My heart raced as I recognized the tension in the air. A young man was pacing back and forth with a frantic expression. I motioned for Hannah to stay back as I approached the crowd.

"Hey, what happened?" I asked while trying to keep my voice calm.

The man turned to me with desperation in his eyes. "There was a shooting. A couple of blocks down. I saw someone get hit!" His voice shook as he spoke and I could see the fear etched on his face.

"Are the police on the way?" I pressed as my mind raced.

"Yeah, I called them but they're taking forever," he replied while glancing nervously down the street.

I turned back to Hannah who had followed me closer than I intended. "We need to get to safety. Let's move back toward the apartment," I said as my protective instincts flared.

"No," she insisted. "We can't just leave. What if someone needs help?"

I hesitated. I was caught between my instinct to shield her and her determination to help. "Hannah, we don't know what we're walking into. Please, let's go."

However, her eyes were resolute. I realized that this was part of who she was. She was someone who cared deeply for others and she was willing to step into danger if it meant helping someone in need. I sighed as the weight of our connection grounded me.

"Okay, but we have to be careful," I relented. My heart was pounding as I led the way back toward the chaos.

As we neared the scene, the flashing lights of police cars began to illuminate the street. They cutting through the darkness like beacons of authority. Officers were directing traffic. Their presence was a stark reminder of the reality we were facing.

"Stay close to me," I instructed with my instincts on high alert.

Hannah nodded. Her eyes darted around as we approached the perimeter established by the police. I could see the outline of a figure on the ground. It was surrounded by emergency personnel. My heart sank at the sight; this was a real and raw reminder of the unpredictability of life.

"Is everyone okay?" I asked an officer who was directing the crowd.

"Just stay back, folks. We're handling it," he replied curtly. He was focused on his task.

The gravity of the situation settled over us like a heavy blanket. I felt Hannah's hand slip into mine. This small gesture of solidarity grounded me in the chaos.

"Look," she whispered. "There's someone over there who looks like they might need help." She pointed toward a woman sitting on the sidewalk. Her face was pale. She was shaken up.

Instinctively, I moved toward the woman with Hannah beside me. "Ma'am, are you alright?" I asked while kneeling down to her level.

The woman looked up with tears streaming down her cheeks. "I—I saw everything. I didn't know what to do," she stammered in a whisper.

"We're here now," Hannah said gentle while kneeling beside me. "Can you tell us what happened?"

As the woman recounted the events, I felt a mixture of anger and sorrow well up inside me. The senselessness of violence and the fragility of life rushed back to me like a wave. I struggled to keep my composure.

"Help is on the way," I assured her. "You're going to be okay."

The sirens wailed in the distance. I glanced at Hannah's expression of empathy and strength. In that moment, I knew we were in this together—no matter the outcome.

As the paramedics arrived, I stood back and allowed them to take over. The urgency of the situation shifted my focus. It was a reminder of my role as an officer. However, I couldn't shake the feeling of vulnerability that accompanied Hannah's presence. She was here. She was standing by me in the face of chaos and it both terrified and exhilarated me.

Once the paramedics had taken control, I turned to Hannah. "You were incredible back there."

She smiled softly. The warmth of her presence cut through the tension. "I just wanted to help. It's what we do, right?"

"Yeah, it is," I said as my heart swelled with admiration.

As we stepped back into the shadows, the night felt different. The uncertainty of what laid ahead lingered, but the bond we shared had deepened.

"Let's head back," I suggested as I felt the weight of the night settle around us.

"Together," she replied.

Hand in hand, we walked back toward the light of her apartment. We were ready to face whatever new beginnings awaited us.

7

RECKONING

The morning sun barely kissed the horizon when I received the call that would change everything. I was being promoted to a special assignment: a task force. Excitement surged through me, but it came with a weight that was a reminder of the responsibility that now rested on my shoulders. As I walked through the precinct, my colleagues clapped me on the back while their cheers echoed in my ears. I knew this was just the beginning of a new work chapter.

That evening, my new partner, Officer Brown, was waiting for me at a local bar with an infectious grin. "Welcome to the team, Nigeria! We're celebrating your promotion tonight!" he declared while raising his glass high.

The bar buzzed with laughter and the clinking of glasses. This familiar atmosphere wrapped around me like a warm blanket. I joined in the revelry as each drink eased the tension that had built up over the past few weeks. As I laughed and toasted with Brown, thoughts of Hannah flitted through my mind. I thought about her laughter and the way her eyes sparkled with passion. Even as the drinks blurred the edges of my vision, just the thought of her made me smile.

As the night wore on, however, a nagging thought settled in the back of my mind. I needed to get home. The drinks had taken their toll and I felt the effects creeping in. "Alright, guys, I think I'm calling it a night," I announced as my voice slightly slurred.

"Come on, just one more!" Brown insisted, but I shook my head. I had someone important to talk to.

Outside, the cool night air hit me like a splash of cold water. I fumbled for my phone. My fingers danced nervously over the screen until I found Hannah's name. Dialing her number ignited a rush of anticipation within me.

As the first ring echoed in my ear, I felt a surge of excitement that made me lose focus on the road. I looked up and my heart dropped. I was on the wrong side of the street as headlights glared at me from an oncoming car. Panic surged through my veins as I swerved sharply and narrowly avoided a head-on collision.

I pulled over, My hands were shaking as I gripped the steering wheel. For a moment, my life flashed before my eyes—the choices I'd made, the oaths I'd taken, and the people I cared about. I was lucky. Too lucky. The realization hit me hard; I could have taken a life or lost my own.

Taking a few deep breaths, I returned Hannah's call and attempted to mask the turmoil that churned within me. "Hey, David! Is everything okay?" she asked. Her voice was bright yet laced with concern.

"Yeah, everything's fine," I replied while trying to sound casual, but I could hear the tension in my own voice.

"Are you sure? You sound a bit off," she noted. She was perceptive as ever.

I hesitated with the weight of the night crashing down. "I just had a long day. You know, the promotion and all," I said with a hope to brush it off.

"Where are you now?" she pressed. "Let me come and pick you up!"

"No, really, I'm okay," I insisted as the false sense of security from the drinks whispered in my ear. I couldn't let her worry.

"Don't lie to me, David. You're my friend. Just tell me what happened," she urged. Her voice was firm yet gentle.

I took a deep breath as the reality of the situation settled heavily on my chest. "I was just driving home and I wasn't paying attention. I almost... I almost got into an accident."

There was a pause on the other end and I could almost feel her concern wrapping around me like a blanket. "Oh my God. Are you serious? Are you hurt?"

"No, I'm fine. I pulled over to the side," I said with guilt creeping in. "But I shouldn't have been driving. I had a few drinks to celebrate."

"Why would you risk that?" she asked as her voice edged with worry. "You took an oath to protect lives, David. Not just others', but your own too."

Her words hit me hard. I had a duty, not just to my job, but to myself and the people I cared about. "I know, I know," I replied as my voice lowered. "I messed up."

"Where are you now?" she asked again. Her tone was softer but still insistent. "Let me come and get you."

"I'm fine. Really," I said. However, the truth hung heavy in the air. I was still shaken but the impaired judgment gave me a false sense of control. "I just need to go home and think."

After I hung up, I sat in my car and stared into the darkness of the night. I replayed the events of the day in my mind: the thrill of my promotion, the celebration at the bar, and the reckless decision to drive while buzzed. The weight of my choices pressed down on me and mixed with the disappointment I felt in myself.

I had taken an oath to uphold the law, protect, and serve. Yet, here I was, almost taking a life because I couldn't make a responsible choice. The thrill of the day had turned into a stark reminder of how quickly everything could change.

As I drove home, the city lights blurred past me. The kaleidoscope of colors intermingled with the weight of my thoughts. I had been given a chance to make a difference and I almost threw it away. I would have to do better, not just for myself, but for the people who believed in me, especially Hannah.

This wasn't just a new beginning—it was a reckoning. I faced it head-on. I started with a promise to myself: never again would I let a moment of celebration cloud my judgment. I was lucky that night, but I wouldn't push my luck again.

8

FRACTURED

This title captures the emotional turmoil of the chapter. It highlights both the personal growth and the tension in Officer Nigeria's relationship with Hannah. It reflects the dual themes of redemption and the fragility of connections in the face of challenges.

The morning light seeped through my curtains and illuminated the remnants of last night's mistakes. I rubbed my temples as I tried to shake off the lingering effects of the alcohol and the weight of regret that sat heavily on my chest. The thrill of my promotion felt like a distant memory now. It was overshadowed by the tight knot of anxiety that twisted in my gut. I had promised myself a reckoning but the clarity of morning brought its own set of challenges.

An unexpected message broke through the haze: "Nigeria, we need to talk. Meet me at the precinct." It was from Captain Smith. My stomach churned. I had no doubt this was about my reckless decision to drive home.

As I drove to the precinct, each stoplight felt like a countdown to judgment day. I replayed the night in my mind: the laughter of my colleagues, the clinking of glasses, and the thrill of celebration morphing into a chilling realization of how close I had come to disaster. My heart raced as I parked. The weight of my actions pressed down on me like a lead blanket.

The air inside the precinct was thick with tension. My colleagues buzzed around me with cheerful yet distant voices. Their world was detached from my inner turmoil. As I stepped into Captain Smith's office, the door closed behind me with a definitive thud that sealed me in a room filled with looming consequences.

"Sit," Captain Smith commanded. His tone brokered no argument.

I took a seat, with the weight of my actions crashing down again. "I know why I'm here," I said in a voice that was barely above a whisper. Shame washed over me and left me exposed.

"Do you?" he replied while arching an eyebrow. "Because it seems to me like you're on a fast track to jeopardizing, not just your career, but the lives of others. Do you understand what could have happened?"

I nodded as thick and suffocating guilt flooding my senses. "I messed up, sir. I shouldn't have driven. I should have called someone."

"Exactly," he said while leaning back in his chair as his gaze pierced through me. "But this isn't just about you. You're now part of a special task force where lives are at stake. Your decisions affect your partner, your team, and the community. You need to internalize that."

His words echoed in my mind and punctured the bubble of denial that I had wrapped around myself. "I understand, Captain. It won't happen again," I replied, but the conviction in my voice felt hollow.

"Good. But understanding isn't enough. I want you to spend some time in community outreach and working with at-risk youth. Show them that choices have consequences, and that you're not above the law. You're on probation for the next month."

The shock of his words hit me like a punch to the gut. Community outreach? It felt like a blow, but I also recognized it as an opportunity for redemption. "Yes, sir. I'll do whatever it takes."

"Good. You're a promising officer, Nigeria, but you need to earn back our trust." The weight of his disappointment felt like a shackle around my heart.

As I left Captain Smith's office, uncertainty washed over me like a cold wave. I was no stranger to the streets, but interacting with those who had strayed from the right path would be a different challenge altogether. I had always seen myself as a protector, but now I would be a mentor and a guide. Would they listen to me? Would they see me as a hypocrite and an emblem of the very mistakes I was trying to help them avoid?

Later that day, I met with Officer Brown to discuss the upcoming outreach program. He was supportive, albeit cautious. "This could be good for you, man. But you know they'll see right through you if you're not genuine."

I nodded with gratitude for his honesty. "I just need to figure out how to connect with them. I want to show them that change is possible."

Brown clapped me on the shoulder while grounding me in the moment. "Just be yourself. They'll respect your story if you let them in. And remember, you're not just talking at them; you're sharing with them."

That evening, I called Hannah. I needed her perspective. Her steady presence was a balm to my frayed nerves. "Hey, David! How's it going?" Her voice wrapped around me like a comforting hug.

"I'm... okay. Just dealing with some fallout from last night," I admitted as my heart pounded with a mix of fear and vulnerability.

"Do you want to talk about it?" she asked gently. Even through the phone, her concern was palpable.

"I have to do community outreach now. It's a punishment, but I guess it's also a chance to make things right." I paused. I was unsure of how she'd respond. "I just feel so... lost."

"Wow, that's a big step. But I think it's a good idea. You have a lot to offer and those kids need role models. Just be real with them," she encouraged. Her unwavering belief in me ignited a spark of determination.

"Thanks, Hannah. I appreciate your support. I'm going to do my best," I replied while feeling a flicker of hope.

As I hung up, I realized that this experience might not only help the youth I'd be working with. It could also be a stepping stone for my own growth. I had a long way to go, but this was my chance to face my reckoning head-on.

The next day, I stepped into the community center with nerves bubbling in my stomach. A group of teenagers lounged around. Their expressions ranged from disinterest to mild curiosity. Before introducing myself, I took a deep breath to steady myself against the tide of uncertainty. "I'm Officer Nigeria, and I'm here to share my story."

Their eyes narrowed and I knew I had to earn their attention. "I want to talk about choices, the good ones and the bad ones. I've made my fair share of mistakes, but I'm here to tell you that it's never too late to turn things around."

As I spoke, I saw their expressions shift from skepticism to engagement. I was no longer just a badge; I was someone who had stumbled but was determined to rise again. I shared my near-miss on the road, the panic that had surged through me, and the shame that followed. I could see the flicker of recognition in their eyes and the understanding that came from shared human experiences.

As I delved deeper into my story, I revealed my fears, my struggles with self-doubt, and my desire to make a difference. "I'm not perfect," I admitted as my voice trembled with emotion. "But I believe in the power of second chances."

The room was silent as the weight of my words hung in the air. I caught a glimpse of a girl in the back whose her arms were crossed tightly against her chest. Her face was etched with defiance. "Why should we listen to you? You almost messed up your life," she shot back in a sharp voice.

I took a deep breath as the sting of her words cut deep. "You're right," I said as my heart raced. "I did mess up. But that's exactly why I'm here. I want to show you that you don't have to make the same mistakes I did. You can choose a different path."

Slowly, I watched as her expression softened. The walls she had built around herself began to crumble. "I'm not here to preach," I continued while steadying my voice. "I'm here to share my journey, and maybe together we can find a better way."

As the session progressed, I felt the barriers between us dissolving. They were being replaced by a fragile trust. We shared laughter, stories, and even some tears. I realized that this wasn't just about me teaching them; it was about all of us learning from one another.

As I wrapped up, I sensed a shift in the room. "Thank you for being honest with us," one boy saiid. His voice was quiet but filled with sincerity. "It's nice to know we're not alone."

For the first time in a long while, I felt a sense of purpose. This was my reckoning, and I was ready to embrace it. The road ahead would be challenging, but I was no longer just a figure of authority; I was a mentor, a friend, and perhaps even a beacon of hope for those who needed it most.

Later that evening, as I drove home, I felt buoyed by the day's events but equally eager to share my experience with Hannah. I dialed her number as my heart raced with anticipation. "Hey, Hannah! Do you want to grab dinner tonight? I'd love to tell you how it went."

"Of course! I can't wait to hear all about it," she replied with an infectious enthusiasm.

We met at our favorite Italian restaurant. The atmosphere was warm and inviting. As we settled into a cozy booth, I recounted my day while feeling a rush of pride and vulnerability. Her eyes sparkled with interest and I could see her processing my journey as the weight of my words resonated with her.

However, as the conversation flowed, a subtle tension began to build. "You know, it's great you're doing this outreach," she said with her brow furrowing slightly. "But I just worry you're putting too much pressure on yourself. You can't save everyone."

I felt a flash of defensiveness. "I'm not trying to save anyone! I'm just trying to show them there's hope. Isn't that worth something?"

Hannah sighed as her expression softened. "I get that, but it doesn't mean you have to carry the entire burden. You need to take care of yourself too, Nigeria. You can't pour from an empty cup."

I leaned back while feeling frustration bubble within me. "I'm trying to be better! I thought you'd be proud of me."

"I am proud," she said. Her voice was steady but tinged with concern. "But I don't want you to lose yourself in the process."

The warmth of the restaurant felt suddenly stifling and I could feel the distance growing between us. "Maybe you just don't understand," I snapped. The words escaped before I could rein them in.

Hannah's eyes widened as hurt flashed across her face. "Maybe I don't," she replied quietly. The air was thick with unspoken words.

We fell into an uncomfortable silence. The clinking of plates and laughter from nearby tables faded into the background. The evening that had begun with promise now felt fraught with tension. Our earlier connection slipped through our fingers like sand.

As we finished dinner, the unresolved disagreement hung heavy between us. I could see the conflict reflected in her eyes. "Can we talk about this later?" she asked in a whisper.

"Yeah, maybe," I replied but uncertainty gnawed at me. I didn't want to leave things unresolved, but I also felt the weight of my own choices pressing down on me.

As we parted outside the restaurant, a chill swept through the air and mirrored the unease that lingered between us. I watched her walk away. Her silhouette grew smaller and my heart became heavier with doubt. What had started off as a day of hope and redemption now felt clouded by a disagreement that left me wondering about the future of our relationship.

What would tomorrow bring? Would we find our way back to each other or had this moment fractured something that couldn't be repaired? As I stood in the cool night air, I felt a sense of foreboding settle in. The road ahead was uncertain. I couldn't shake the feeling that this was just the beginning of a much larger journey.

9

TURNING POINTS

After the dinner with Hannah, I awoke with a sense of unease the following morning. The sun streamed through my window, but it felt muted. It was like the world outside was still processing the weight of last night's unresolved conversation. I tossed and turned while replaying the look on Hannah's face; a mixture of concern and hurt was etched deep into her features.

I had a choice to make: I could either dwell in the discomfort or confront it head-on. A part of me wanted to retreat, bury myself in work, and distance myself from the emotional turmoil. However, the part of me, that had grown stronger through my outreach experience, urged me to take responsibility.

After a quick breakfast, I drove to the community center for another session with the youth. I needed to channel my energy into something positive and show them that facing difficult conversations was a part of growth. As I arrived, a few of the teenagers were already gathered and their chatter filled the room with a sense of anticipation.

"Hey, everyone!" I called while forcing a smile that I hoped would mask the unease I felt inside. "Today, I want to talk about resilience—how we bounce back from setbacks and confront our fears."

The discussion flowed easily as stories of personal challenges and triumphs were shared among the group. I encouraged them to dig deep and explore the moments that tested their resolve. As I listened to their stories, I found myself reflecting on my own. Each tale echoed the themes of vulnerability and strength I had experienced recently.

After the session, I felt invigorated but the nagging worry about Hannah still lingered at the back of my mind. I needed to reach out and clear the air. I grabbed my phone. My fingers hovered over her contact as hesitated to press call. Despite, I couldn't let fear dictate the conversation.

"Hey, Hannah. Can we talk? I want to clear the air about last night," I texted. My heart raced as I hit send.

The minutes felt like hours. My anxiety mounted with each passing moment. When my phone finally buzzed, I nearly dropped it. "I'd like that. Can we meet at our usual spot?"

A wave of relief washed over me but the tension was still palpable. I needed to approach this conversation with care. I had to be open and honest about my feelings without getting defensive. As I drove to our meeting place, I rehearsed what I wanted to say and tried to quell the doubt that crept in.

When I arrived, Hannah was already there. She was sitting at our favorite table by the window. The moment I saw her, a pang of regret washed over me. Even in her quiet contemplation, she looked beautiful. However, there was an unmistakable shadow in her eyes.

"Hey," I said softly as I sat down. The weight of the unspoken hung between us.

"Hey," she replied in a whisper.

We sat in silence for a moment as the noise of the café faded into the background. I wanted to reach across the table, take her hand, and remind her that we were still connected despite our differences. However, I held back. I was unsure of how to bridge the gap.

"I've been thinking about what you said last night," I began. My voice was steady despite the turmoil inside. "I realize that I've been so focused on trying to make a difference that I may have overlooked how this affects me—and us."

Hannah looked up. Her eyes searched mine. "I didn't mean to make you feel like you had to choose. I just want you to be okay."

"I know, and I appreciate that," I replied as my heart swelled with gratitude. "But I also want to be honest with you. Helping those kids means a lot to me. It's not just a job; it's personal. I want to show them there's hope, even when it feels like there isn't."

As I spoke, I felt the weight of my words hanging in the air. I could see her processing everything as her brows knitted together in thought. "I get that. But you have to take care of yourself too. You can't pour from an empty cup."

Her concern wrapped around me like a warm blanket, but it also made me realize the chasm between my dedication and the toll it was taking on my personal life. "I'm learning that," I admitted. "And I want to find a balance. I don't want to lose you in the process."

Hannah's expression softened. For the first time since our conversation the night before, I saw a glimmer of hope in her eyes. "Then let's work on that together. I want to support you, but I also want you to be honest with me about how you're feeling."

I smiled as I felt the tension ease just a little. "I can do that. I really want us to work. It's just... it's been a lot to navigate."

"Life's messy," she said as a small smile broke through her uncertainty. "But I'm here for you."

As we continued to talk, I could feel the bond between us strengthening. I left the café with a renewed sense of purpose and gratitude for the connection we'd managed to rekindle.

Returning to work later that day, I felt a renewed energy course through me. It was a relief to know I was off probation. This milestone marked both my professional and personal growth. I stepped into the familiar chaos of the office as I was greeted by the sounds of ringing phones and clattering keyboards.

"Hey, Nigeria!" my captain called from across the room. His voice cut through the din. "Got a minute?"

I walked over with an eagerness to share the experiences that had shaped me during my time off. "Absolutely, Captain. I just had a breakthrough discussion."

As I recounted the morning's revelations and my commitment to balance my work and personal life, I felt the weight of my journey settle comfortably on my shoulders. There was still work to do, but I was ready to face it with Hannah by my side and a clearer understanding of myself.

As I spoke, I realized that each turning point and every conversation was just another step toward becoming the person I aspired to be. The chapter was closing, but the story was far from over.

10

THE LONGEST RUN

The sun was just peeking over the horizon as I laced up my running shoes. The cool morning air filled my lungs with a sense of possibility. I had always found solace in the rhythm of my feet hitting the pavement. This was a meditative escape from the chaos of life. As I set out on my usual route, the familiar streets felt reassuring. They were a comforting backdrop to the growing uncertainty in my heart.

That morning, as I rounded the corner near the park, my phone buzzed violently in my pocket. I pulled it out and glanced at the caller ID. It was my captain. The knot in my stomach tightened. Something felt wrong.

"Nigeria!" my captain's voice crackled through the line as urgency laced his words. "We've got a situation. Officer Reyes was involved in a shooting. It doesn't look good."

Time froze. The world around me blurred as his words sank in. "What do you mean? Where is he?" I stammered while panic rose in my chest.

"He's at the hospital. Just get there as fast as you can," he said. The gravity of his tone sent chills down my spine.

I didn't think; I just ran. I pushed myself harder than I ever had before. Each breath was a desperate plea for time to stand still. My legs burned and my heart raced, but I didn't stop. I couldn't. I had to get to Reyes.

When I arrived at the hospital, the sterile smell of antiseptic hit me like a wall. I rushed through the doors as my heart pounded in my chest. I searched for anyone who could tell me where he was. The chaos of the emergency room swirled around me, but all I could hear was the echo of my captain's voice.

"Officer Reyes's family is in the waiting room," a nurse said with a somber expression. My stomach dropped. I knew what that meant.

As I walked toward the waiting area, the sight of his family gathered together was a gut-wrenching reminder of the fragility of life. I was met by his wife, whose eyes were red and swollen from tears, and his children, who clung to her side. Confusion was etched across their faces. Colleagues of ours stood nearby. Their expressions were grave and the air was thick with unspoken grief.

I approached them but the words got caught in my throat. I wanted to offer comfort but my heart felt heavy with despair. Reyes was gone. Just like that.

The realization hit me like a tidal wave and I felt myself slip into a numbness I had never experienced before. I stood there, frozen, as the world continued to spin around me. The laughter of children and the beeping of machines all faded into a dull hum. I felt hollow The essence of who I was had been stripped away.

From that day forward, I was never the same. My heart hardened and violence became the new normal. I attended the funeral. I stood in a sea of black while surrounded by mourners who felt the same crushing loss. It was a hollow ceremony. This final goodbye felt inadequate for a man who had meant so much to so many.

After the funeral, I sought refuge in the one thing that had always been there for me—the bottle. It was easy to drown out the pain and numb the ache that clawed at my insides. Days turned into a blur as I avoided Hannah and everyone else who tried to reach out. I couldn't bear their concern or their attempts to help me. I didn't want help; I wanted to escape.

As the weeks dragged on, I felt my empathy and sympathy slip away with every arrest I made. Each time I put handcuffs on someone, I felt less. I became a machine that was going through the motions as my heart became encased in a fortress of indifference. Interactions with the community no longer felt meaningful. Instead, they were overshadowed by the weight of my grief.

Days turned into weeks and weeks into months. I created a routine that revolved around the bottle. I needed a drink every morning to kick-start my day and another every night to quiet the demons that haunted me. The familiar burn of alcohol became my only solace. It was a twisted comfort that masked the reality I couldn't face.

In the solitude of my apartment, I sank deeper into my own despair. I was surrounded by empties that mirrored the emptiness I felt inside. I lost track of time and myself. The man who had once fought for hope and change was now a shadow of his former self. I was adrift in a sea of numbness and trapped in a cycle of self-destruction.

As much as I tried to drown it out, the reality remained: I was alone and I couldn't escape the darkness that had settled in my soul.

11

THE BOTTLE'S EMBRACE

The morning light seeped through the blinds like unwelcome intruders and illuminated the chaos of empty bottles that littered my living room. I laid sprawled on the couch as the remnants of last night's drinking clung to me like a heavy fog. Today was supposed to be the first day of an outreach program that was a chance to honor Reyes's legacy, but the thought of facing a room full of eager faces felt impossibly heavy.

Instead, I chose the bottle.

I poured myself a drink and let the amber liquid wash over my tongue like a warm embrace. Each sip numbed the pain and drowned out the memories of Reyes and the weight of my guilt. I lost track of time in the haze of alcohol. The world outside faded into a distant murmur.

Hours later, as I was sprawled out on the couch, a sharp knock at the door jolted me awake. I groaned as the sound pierced through the fog of my mind.

"Who is it?" I croaked in a voice that was barely audible.

"It's Hannah!" came the familiar voice that was bright yet filled with concern. "Open the door!"

"Go home, Hannah. I don't want to talk," I mumbled as curling into the cushions and hoped she would just leave.

"I'll be right here until you open the door," she replied in an unwavering tone.

Hours ticked by and her soft knock became a steady reminder of my reality. I could hear her encouraging words filtering through my stupor and urging me to let her in. "Remember the first time we met? You came into my office looking like you'd just walked out of a storm."

Her voice painted a picture in my mind and I couldn't help but reminisce. I had been a mess that day. I was overwhelmed and unsure of myself. Hannah had greeted me with a warm smile and her presence calmed the storm inside of me. She had a way of making me feel seen. She knew how to pull me back from the edge.

"Come on, David," she continued. Her voice was gentle, yet persistent. "You can't shut me out forever. I'm here for you. Just think about how far you've come since that first meeting."

I could feel the walls I had built around myself starting to crack. The memory of her kindness stirred something deep within me—a flicker of the hope I thought I had lost.

Finally, with a reluctant sigh, I swung the door open.

"You always had a way of tricking me into doing something I didn't want to do," I blurted out as the alcohol dulled my filter.

Hannah stepped inside. Her expression was a mix of relief and concern. "I just want to help, David."

I shook my head with anger boiling to the surface. "You never wanted to be with me. It was all a part of your job. You were just being nice to me to say, 'Look, here's another one I helped.' I guess that's what all psychiatrists do."

The words tumbled out. They were fueled by a mixture of hurt and alcohol. I watched her face fall in response to my sentiments. I could see the pain in her eyes, and for a moment, I regretted my outburst.

"Is that really how you see me?" she asked softly with hurt lacing her voice. "You think I don't care?"

"No, David," she replied. "I see you as a person. Someone I care about deeply. I'm not here because of my job. I'm here because I want to be."

As the truth of her words settled in, I felt the weight of my accusations begin to crumble. I wanted to believe her but the alcohol clouded my judgment. I turned away.

"Just... just go," I mumbled as I sank back onto the couch.

However, Hannah didn't budge. Instead, she moved closer. Her presence grounded me. "I'm not leaving you like this. I'll stay until you're ready to talk."

Hours passed. Despite my best efforts to shut her out, I found myself drawn to her. She sat on the floor and recounted stories of her experiences. Each word pulled me back from the precipice of despair. Slowly, I began to open up and share fragments of my pain, regrets, and the darkness I had been drowning in.

As the night wore on, I could feel the heaviness in my heart begin to lift, just a little. It was a small step, but it was a step forward. I realized that perhaps I didn't have to face this darkness alone. Hannah had become a new ally in a battle I thought I had to fight all by myself.

As the shadows of the past began to recede, I could finally see a glimmer of light ahead.

12

A NEW BEGINNING

The sun hung low in the sky and casted a golden glow over the city as I walked hand-in-hand with Hannah through the park. It had been months since that fateful night when she refused to leave my side. In that time, we had rebuilt what had been broken between us. With each passing day, our connection deepened and the walls I had built around my heart slowly crumbled.

Hannah turned to me as her eyes sparkled with warmth. "Can you believe how far we've come?" she asked. Her voice was soft and filled with wonder.

I smiled as I recalled the darkness that had once enveloped me. "I honestly didn't think I'd be here, with you, feeling this way again," I admitted. "You've brought light back into my life, Hannah."

She squeezed my hand tighter. "And you've shown me what it means to be loved deeply. I never knew how much I needed you until I found you again."

We stopped beneath a sprawling oak tree. Its branches danced gently in the breeze. I could feel the weight of the moment pressing down on me and urging me to express everything I felt. I took a deep breath with my heart racing as I reached into my pocket.

"Hannah," I began. My voice was trembling with emotion. "From the first moment we met, you saw me for who I really am. You pulled me back from the edge when I thought there was no way out. I can't imagine my life without you. You're my partner, my confidante, and my best friend."

She looked up at me. Her eyes were wide and I could see the surprise mixed with anticipation.

"I want to build a future with you," I continued with my heart pounding as I knelt down on one knee. The ring glinted in the sunlight. "Will you marry me?"

Tears filled her eyes as she gasped. Her hands flew to her mouth. "Oh my God, Nigeria!"

"Say yes," I urged as a smile broke through my nerves. "Please say yes."

"Yes! Yes, of course, I'll marry you!" she exclaimed with laughter and tears as I slipped the ring onto her finger.

In that moment, everything felt perfect. We embraced and the world around us faded away. The chaos of life, the shadows of the past, and the uncertainties of the future melted into a single heartbeat.

As the months rolled by, our love blossomed. We spent lazy Sundays together, exploring the city, cooking meals, and dreaming about what our future would hold. It felt like a fairytale— one that I had never dared to wish for.

Then came the day when Hannah told me the news that would turn our world upside down. "I'm pregnant," she said. Her voice trembled with excitement and fear.

I remember the moment vividly; Time seemed to stand still as the weight of her words settled over us. I pulled her into my arms and spun her around as joy bubbled up inside me. "We're going to be parents!" I said as my heart soared.

As the months passed, we prepared for our child: we painted the nursery, picked out names, and imagined the life we would build together. Our bond grew stronger. Each moment was filled with the kind of laughter and love that made time feel infinite.

On a seemingly ordinary day at work, a phone call came that shattered the calm. I was mid-conversation with a colleague when my phone buzzed insistently. The caller ID made my heart drop—Hannah's doctor.

"Officer Nigeria," the voice on the other end said. It was urgent and professional. "Your wife is in labor. You need to get to the hospital immediatcly."

Panic surged through me. "Is she okay? How far along is she?"

"She's stable but things are progressing quickly. You need to hurry."

I hung up. Adrenaline coursed through my veins as I sprinted to the parking lot. My mind raced with thoughts of Hannah, our child, and the future we had dreamed of together. I couldn't shake the fear that gripped me—what if something went wrong?

As I drove, every red light felt like a lifetime. I could almost hear the rhythmic sound of her breathing and the way she would look at me with that mix of determination and love. I envisioned her in that hospital room: a warrior about to bring our child into the world.

Finally, I burst through the hospital doors as my heart pounded in my chest. I rushed to the front desk. My breath came in quick gasps. "Hannah Nigeria—where is she?" I demanded.

"Room 302," the nurse replied. Her expression was calm amidst the chaos.

I dashed down the hallway as the sounds of machines and hurried footsteps echoed around me. I reached her room and pushed the door open. My heart was in my throat.

There she was, lying on the bed, as sweat glistened on her forehead. Her face showed a mixture of pain and resolve. When she saw me, a smile broke through the tension. "David!" she gasped while reaching for me.

I rushed to her side and took her hand in mine. "I'm here. I'm right here," I whispered as my voice thickened with emotion.

"I can't do this without you," she said as her grip tightened around my fingers.

"You're the strongest person I know. You can do this," I assured her while brushing a stray hair from her face. "We're in this together."

As the waves of labor hit her, I held her hand and grounded her with every breath. We were a team and family. Nothing was going to tear us apart.

With each contraction, I watched Hannah summon every ounce of strength buried within her. It was a beautiful and terrifying process. I marveled at her resilience. The doctor entered and the room filled with the electric energy of impending life.

"Hannah, you're doing amazing," I said in a steady voice filled with love and encouragement.

Finally, after what felt like an eternity, the moment arrived. With one final push, a cry pierced through the air—the sound of our child taking its first breath. Tears streamed down my face as the doctor placed our baby on Hannah's chest.

"It's a girl," the doctor announced and I couldn't contain my joy.

Hannah looked down at our daughter as her eyes shined with tears of happiness. "Our little miracle," she whispered in a voice filled with awe.

I leaned down and kissed Hannah as I was overwhelmed with love. "I can't believe we did it."

"We did," she replied with a radiant smile. "And I couldn't have done it without you."

In that moment, everything felt right in the world. We were no longer just David and Hannah; we were a family that was bound together by love and hope. We were ready to face whatever came next. As I held my wife and our newborn daughter, I knew our story was just beginning. I couldn't wait to see where it would take us.

13

THE JOURNEY AHEAD

The hospital room was filled with a gentle hush. The only sounds were the soft beeping of machines and the rhythmic cooing of our newborn daughter. I sat beside Hannah with my heart overflowing as I watched her cradle our little girl. Hannah's eyes were filled with a love that radiated warmth and peace.

"Can you believe she's finally here?" Hannah whispered while glancing up at me with tears of joy shimmering in her eyes.

I shook my head in awe. "It feels surreal. I didn't think I could love someone this much."

As our daughter nestled closer against Hannah's chest, I felt an overwhelming sense of responsibility wash over me. This tiny being was ours and with that came a promise to protect her, nurture her, and give her a life filled with love and joy.

"What should we name her?" Hannah asked in soft voice. It was as if she were afraid to break the spell of this moment.

I had thought about this countless times. "How about Mia? It means 'mine'—a perfect way to describe how I feel about her."

"Mia," Hannah repeated with a smile blooming on her face. "I love it. Mia Nigeria has a nice ring to it."

We both laughed. The sound echoed in the quiet room and filled it with warmth. It felt like a new chapter was beginning, not just for Mia, but for us as a family.

As the hours passed, visitors came and went as they showered us with love and support. Our friends and family filled the room with laughter and congratulations. Amidst the joy, I found myself retreating into my thoughts. I couldn't shake the weight of my past: the shadows that still lurked at the edges of my mind.

Later that evening, after everyone had left, I sat beside Hannah as she gently rocked Mia to sleep. The soft glow of the bedside lamp illuminated her features. Even in the exhaustion of new motherhood, I couldn't help but admire how beautiful she looked.

"Hannah," I said slowly, "I want to talk about something."

Her brow furrowed with concern, but she nodded and encouraged me to continue.

"I know things have changed, and I should be happy. I am happy, but I'm also scared. Scared that I won't be the father she needs, that I'll slip back into old habits, that I won't be able to protect you both."

Hannah looked at me. Her expression was steady and resolute. "Nigeria, you're not alone in this. We're a team. We've faced the darkness together and we can face whatever comes next. You've come so far. Don't underestimate how strong you are."

"I just don't want to let you down," I admitted. My voice was thick with emotion.

"You won't," she promised as her hand rested on mine. "You've already proven to me how much you care. Just be present. That's all Mia needs."

As the night wore on, I found myself lost in thought and reflecting on my journey. The shadows of my past were still there, but I had a choice. I could let them define my future or I could fight for the happiness I had found with Hannah and Mia.

In the days that followed, we settled into a routine that felt both comforting and chaotic. Each morning, I would wake early to help Hannah with Mia. I learned to change diapers and soothe her cries. Our little girl became the center of our world. With every coo and smile, I felt my heart expand.

However, as the weeks passed, I struggled with the weight of my responsibilities. I wanted to be the perfect husband and father, but the fear of failure loomed over me. I found myself retreating more often and seeking solace in solitude. I began slipping back into old habits of isolation.

One night, after a particularly tough day, I found myself sitting on the porch and staring into the darkness. The bottle sat nearby; it was a familiar temptation that whispered to me. Just one drink, I thought, to take the edge off.

However, as I reached for it, a small voice interrupted my thoughts. "Dad?" Mia's soft cry came from inside and I froze.

In that instant, I realized what I was about to do. I couldn't let the shadows win. I stood up, took a deep breath, and walked back inside.

Hannah was rocking Mia gently in her arms. "I heard her," I said. "I'm here."

She looked up at me with concern etched in her features. "Are you okay?"

"I'm working on it," I replied while taking a seat beside her. "I just... I don't want to let you down. I want to be better for you both."

"You're already doing it," she said softly. "Just by being here and choosing us, you're doing better than you realize."

As I looked at my wife and daughter, I felt a renewed determination surge within me. I had fought through the darkness before and I could do it again. This time, I wouldn't face it alone.

"I love you both," I said. My voice was filled with conviction. "I'm going to make this work. Together."

Hannah smiled. "Together."

In that moment, I knew that while the journey ahead would be challenging, it would also be filled with love, laughter, and the strength of our bond. I had a family now and I was ready to embrace every moment of this new beginning.

14

THE STRENGTH OF FAMILY

T he sound of a soft giggle echoed through the house and cut through the morning stillness like a spark of light in the dark. I awoke to the sweet melody of Mia's laughter: a sound that filled my heart with warmth and purpose. It was a reminder that each day was a new chance to embrace the joy that had entered our lives.

I rubbed the sleep from my eyes and shuffled into the nursery. The scent of baby powder and fresh linens wrapped around me like a comforting blanket. There was Hannah, radiant as ever, sitting in the rocking chair and gently swaying back and forth with Mia cradled in her arms. The sunlight streamed in through the window and casted a golden glow around them. That made the moment feel almost ethereal.

"Good morning, beautiful," I said. My voice was husky with sleep.

Hannah looked up and smiled as her eyes sparkled with happiness. "Morning! Someone was very chatty this morning," she replied while glancing down at our daughter who was cooing and reaching for the colorful mobile above her crib.

I stepped closer. I was unable to resist the urge to scoop Mia into my arms. As I did, she looked up at me. Her big eyes were filled with curiosity. "How's my little explorer today?" I asked as I kissed her forehead.

"Ready for an adventure, I think," Hannah said with a playful grin. "What do you have in mind?"

"Let's take her for a walk in the park," I suggested. The thought ignited a spark of excitement in my chest. "Show her the world outside our little bubble."

"Sounds perfect," Hannah replied as her smile widened. "I'll grab the diaper bag."

While she prepared Mia, I took a moment to reflect on how far we had come. This wasn't the life I had envisioned during the darker days, but it was everything I had ever wanted. The laughter, the love, and the little moments like this filled me with newfound strength.

As we made our way to the park, the sun rose higher and casted a warm glow over the neighborhood. The air was crisp and filled with the scent of blooming flowers and freshly cut grass. I pushed the stroller as Hannah walked beside me. Her presence was a steady anchor.

"This is amazing," I said while glancing over at her. "I never knew how fulfilling this would be."

Hannah looked at me as her eyes softened. "It's a journey we're on together, David. Every day will have its challenges, but we'll face them as a family."

Her words resonated deep within me and I felt a rush of determination. I had fought through darkness before and I would do it again if it meant protecting the love we had built.

As we reached the park, I felt a wave of nostalgia wash over me. I had spent countless hours here as a child. I would play on the swings and dream about the future. Now, I stood beside my wife and watched as she gently lifted Mia from the stroller and showed her the vibrant flowers and the playful squirrels darting about.

"Look, Mia! There's a squirrel!" Hannah exclaimed while pointing excitedly.

Mia's eyes widened, and for a moment, I saw the world through her innocent gaze. Everything was new and magical. I couldn't help but smile. I knew that I wanted to be the one to guide her through these moments. I wanted to be her protector and teacher.

As the sun began to set and cast a warm glow over the park, Hannah turned to me. Her expression was serious, yet loving. "I want to talk about something," she said in a steady voice.

"Of course," I replied as heart quickened.

"I know things aren't always easy and I see the weight you carry. I want you to know that I'm here for you, no matter what," she said. Her words wrapped around me like a lifeline.

I took a deep breath while feeling the weight of her concern. "I'm still learning, Hannah. There are days when the shadows creep back in, but I promise I'll keep fighting for us."

"You don't have to fight alone," she said softly while placing a hand on my arm. "We're in this together. We always will be."

In that moment, I felt a surge of love for her so profound that it took my breath away. I leaned down and brushed my lips against hers. A promise was sealed in that tender kiss.

As we made our way back home, I knew the road ahead would have its ups and downs; however, with Hannah and Mia by my side, I felt an unshakeable strength. We were a family that was bound together by love and ready to face whatever challenges laid ahead.

For the first time in a long time, I felt truly hopeful about the future.

15

THE CRACKS BENEATH THE SURFACE

The days had turned into weeks and I was determined to keep my promise to Hannah. I had vowed to fight the shadows that threatened to creep back into my life, but as the nights wore on, I found myself slipping back into old habits. I'd become a master at concealing my drinking by hiding empty bottles in the back of the trash can and masking the smell with mints and gum.

It was a delicate balancing act, and with each passing day, the lie felt heavier. I could see the concern in Hannah's eyes, but I didn't want to burden her with my struggles. She had already given me so much; I didn't want to let her down again.

One evening, after a long shift at work, I returned home with the familiar urge to escape reality. I had spent the night at the bar with my partner. We laughed and drank too much, but it was easier to pretend that everything was fine than to face the truth.

Hannah had already gone to bed when I got home. As I laid beside her and tried to shake off the lingering effects of the alcohol, I felt the weight of my decisions pressing down on me.

"Honey?" she said softly to break the silence. "Can I ask you something without you getting upset?"

I turned to her as my curiosity piqued. "Sure, what's on your mind?"

"You know how much I love you, right? You know how much I care for you," she continued. Her voice was steady, yet tinged with worry. "Is there something you'd like to share with me?"

Confusion washed over me. "No, baby, what's the problem?" I asked while trying to keep my tone light.

Her gaze was unwavering. "I found an empty bottle of liquor in the trash."

My heart raced and panic set in. I hadn't expected her to discover my secret so soon. In that moment, I felt the world tilt beneath me. "Oh, honey, that was old," I lied while forcing a smile that felt more like a grimace. "I was cleaning out the closet. You know how cluttered it gets."

I thought I had reassured her, but who was I really fooling? The look on her face told me everything; she wasn't convinced. I could see the hurt and confusion in her eyes; however, I was too caught in my web of deception to confess the truth.

As the days went on, I found myself gravitating back to the bar after work. I started seeking the comfort of familiarity and the numbing effects of alcohol. I continued to mask the odor with candy and gum. I convinced myself that I was in control. Despite, deep down, I knew I was spiraling again.

Hannah continued trying to reach out by asking me if I was okay, but I brushed her off and told her I was just tired from work. The more I distanced myself, the more the weight of my choices wore down on me. I could see her concern growing, but I was too ashamed to let her in.

It all came to a head one night as I laid in bed while the room spun around me. I felt a sharp pain in my side. This discomfort had crept up on me slowly, but now it was impossible to ignore. I tried to brush it off. I hoped it was just a result of the drinking. Unfortunately, as the days turned into weeks, the pain became more persistent.

Finally, I decided to see a doctor. The waiting room was sterile and quiet. This was a stark contrast to the chaos in my mind. When I was called in, I sat across from the doctor and tried to mask my anxiety with a casual demeanor.

"Mr. Nigeria," he began while flipping through my chart. "We need to discuss some of the test results."

I felt my heart drop. "What's going on?"

The doctor looked at me with a serious expression. "You're experiencing some concerning symptoms. We need to run a few more tests to determine the cause of the pain in your side."

My mind raced as fear gripped me. I had known this day might come but I had hoped to avoid it. I looked out the window and tried to gather my thoughts, but all I could see was the reflection of my own uncertainty staring back at me.

"Is it serious?" I finally managed to ask. My voice was barely above a whisper.

"We'll know more after the tests," he replied. His tone was neutral but the gravity of his words hung heavily in the air.

As I left the office, the weight of the world settled onto my shoulders. I had tried so hard to hide my struggles, but now it felt as if everything was unraveling. I couldn't shake the feeling that my choices were catching up with me. I was left wondering what the future held.

Would I be able to face Hannah with the truth? Would I be strong enough to fight whatever was coming? As I stepped into the parking lot, I realized that I was at a crossroads. I couldn't hide from the consequences of my actions any longer.

The uncertainty loomed large and I knew I had to confront my demons—before it was too late.

16

THE WEIGHT OF TRUTH

The days that followed my visit to the doctor felt like an eternity. Each moment was steeped in tension. The looming fear of what the tests might reveal hung over me like a dark cloud. I tried to maintain a sense of normalcy at home, but every time I looked at Hannah, I felt the weight of my secrets pressing down on me.

She was doing her best to be supportive by asking about my day and checking in on me, but I could see the concern etched in her expression. It made me feel like a fraud who was hiding the truth behind a mask of reassurance. I knew I needed to come clean, but the thought of disappointing her again made my heart race.

One evening, as we sat together on the couch after putting Mia to bed, the silence between us felt charged. Hannah was flipping through a magazine, but her mind was clearly somewhere else. I could see the worry in her eyes and it gnawed at my insides.

"Hannah," I started. My voice trembled slightly. "Can we talk?"

She looked up. Her expression shifted from distraction to concern. "Of course, David. What's on your mind?"

I took a deep breath as my heart pounded in my chest. "I know you found that empty bottle and I want to be honest with you. Things have been hard for me lately. I thought I could handle it but I'm struggling."

Her eyes widened, and I could see her trying to process my words. "Struggling how?" she asked gently.

"I've been drinking again," I admitted. The words tasted bitter on my tongue. "I thought I could keep it under control but I slipped back into the habit. I didn't want to hurt you or let you down."

"Why didn't you tell me?" she asked. Her voice was steady, but I could see the hurt flickering in her eyes.

"I didn't want to burden you," I confessed with shame flooding through me. "You've been my rock through all of this and I didn't want to add to your worries."

Hannah reached for my hand. Her grip was firm, yet comforting. "David, you're not a burden. We're in this together. You don't have to face this alone."

I nodded with gratitude for her understanding, but the weight of my confession felt heavier than ever. "There's more," I said in a whisper. "I went to the doctor because of the pain in my side."

Her expression shifted as her concern deepened "You said it was an old injury from working out."

"I know," I replied. "But the truth is... I think it's the drinking that's caught up with me. I'm waiting on the lab results."

The air in the room thickened. It was heavy with unspoken fears. I could see her processing my words as the realization of how serious this could be washed over her.

"Are you saying...?" she started. As she spoke, I could see the fear in her eyes. Worry creeped in like a shadow.

"I don't know what it means yet," I said while trying to sound more confident than I felt. "But I'm scared, Hannah. Scared of what they might find. What if it's something serious?"

Just then, the sound of a loud crash echoed from the kitchen and made both of us jump. My heart raced as I shot a glance toward the source of the noise. "What was that?" I asked as adrenaline surged through me.

"I—I don't know," Hannah stammered, her eyes wide.

Without thinking, I jumped to my feet. I was ready to protect my family. But as I moved toward the kitchen, a sense of dread washed over me. The fear of, not just the unknown health issues, but the potential danger lurking in the shadows sent a chill down my spine.

When I reached the kitchen, I found the source of the noise—a stack of plates had fallen from the counter. There was shattered pieces scattered across the floor. Relief flooded through me, but it was short-lived.

"Just the plates," I murmured while trying to catch my breath. However, my heart was still racing. The incident rattled me more than it should have.

"Are you okay?" Hannah asked while following me into the kitchen. Her brow was furrowed with concern.

"Yeah, I'm fine," I lied, but the tremor in my voice betrayed me.

As I bent down to clean up the mess, I felt a sharp pain shoot through my side and I winced. The pain was becoming harder to ignore. It was more insistent. The reality of my situation hit me like a punch to the gut—what if I was losing control, not just over my drinking, but also over my life?

"Let's talk about this more," Hannah said gently while kneeling beside me. "I'm here for you, no matter what happens."

I looked into her eyes. The fear that had gripped me began to soften. It was replaced by a flicker of hope. I knew I had to face this head-on. However, as I gathered the broken pieces of glass, I couldn't shake the feeling that something darker loomed just out of sight.

After we cleaned up, I returned to the living room as my mind raced with questions. What would the tests reveal? Would I be able to fight this battle? Was I already too far gone?

As the night wore on, sleep eluded me. Uncertainty gnawed at my insides. I couldn't let my family down again. The weight of my choices continued to press down on me. The shadows I had fought so hard to escape were creeping back in and I was left wondering if I had the strength to face them once more.

With each tick of the clock, the reality of my situation settled in. I had a decision to make—a choice to confront my demons and seek the support I desperately needed before it was too late. However, as the darkness closed in, I couldn't help but wonder if I was already running out of time.

17

FACING THE ABYSS

The night was long and sleepless. Every tick of the clock amplified my anxiety. My mind raced and swirled with thoughts of the tests, the drinking, and the fear that had taken root in my heart. I laid in bed beside Hannah. Her soft breathing was a reminder of the love that anchored me, yet the shadows of my past loomed larger than ever.

When dawn finally broke, I could see the first rays of sunlight creep through the curtains and cast a warm glow over the room. Instead of comfort, it only intensified the turmoil within me. I had to face the reality of my situation. It felt like I was standing on the edge of an abyss and teetering on the brink of despair.

I slipped out of bed, careful not to wake Hannah, and made my way to the nursery. As I peered through the door, I found Mia sleeping peacefully in her crib. Her tiny chest was rising and falling in the rhythm of innocence. The sight of her brought a rush of warmth to my heart that was a stark contrast to the fear gnawing at my insides.

I couldn't help but feel a surge of love and responsibility wash over me. Mia represented hope, a fresh start, and the future I wanted to build with Hannah. But now, with the weight of my diagnosis looming over me, I felt like I was teetering on the edge of losing everything I held dear.

Just as I poured myself a cup of coffee, my phone buzzed on the counter—a message from the doctor. My heart raced as I fumbled for it. A simple text appeared on the screen: "Please call me when you get a chance. We need to discuss your test results."

The words hit me like a sledgehammer and I felt the ground shift beneath my feet. I took a deep breath and tried to steady myself. I needed to tell Hannah. She deserved to know what was happening, but a part of me hesitated. I didn't want to burden her with my fears, but I couldn't face whatever news awaited me alone.

I walked back to the bedroom as heart pounded. Hannah was still asleep. Her face was serene and untouched by the worries of the world. I gently shook her awake and her eyes fluttered open. They were instantly filled with concern.

"Hey, what's wrong?" she asked while sitting up and rubbing the sleep from her eyes.

"I got a call from the doctor," I said in a whisper. "I need to go in. He has my test results."

Hannah's expression shifted from sleepiness to alarm. "Do you want me to come with you?"

I hesitated as the weight of my decision pressed down on me. "I think I need to do this alone," I replied while trying to sound more confident than I felt. "But I'll call you as soon as I know something."

"Promise me you'll be careful," she said. Her eyes searched mine for reassurance.

"I promise," I said while forcing a smile to ease her worry before I turned and walked out the door.

The drive to the doctor's office felt surreal. The streets were alive with morning activity, but all I could focus on was the heavy knot in my stomach. What if the news was bad? What if I couldn't handle it? The fear was a suffocating presence that wrapped tighter and tighter around my chest with each passing moment.

When I arrived at the office, my hands trembled as I signed in and sat in the waiting room. The minutes dragged on. Each tick of the clock amplified my anxiety. Finally, Dr. Matthews appeared and gestured for me to follow him into his office.

"Thanks for coming in," he said. His tone was serious but compassionate. "I know this is difficult."

I nodded. My throat was dry. "Just tell me what's going on."

He took a seat and opened my chart with a grave expression. "The tests show some concerning results related to your liver function. It appears that your alcohol consumption has taken a toll on your health and we need to address this immediately."

Panic surged through me and I felt the walls of the room close in. "What does that mean?" I asked as my voice raised slightly.

"Your liver is showing signs of damage. If you don't make significant changes, it could lead to serious complications," he said. His tone was neutral but the gravity of his words hung heavily in the air.

"Is there any way to reverse it?" I asked as desperation creeped into my voice.

"There's potential for improvement, but it will require commitment and a lifestyle change," he replied. His tone was firm, yet hopeful. "I can refer you to a counselor who specializes in addiction if you're open to it."

I sat there in stunned silence as the weight of his words crashed over me like a tidal wave. I had thought I could control my drinking, but now I faced the very real possibility that my choices had consequences I couldn't ignore.

When I got home, I found Hannah sitting on the couch. Her expression was a mixture of worry and relief as she saw me walk through the door. "What did the doctor say?" she asked as her voice filled with concern.

I took a deep breath with the fear of disappointing her fighting against the need to be honest. "It's not good," I admitted with a heavy heart. "My liver is damaged from drinking and I need to stop completely."

Tears welled in her eyes. She rushed to my side and wrapped her arms around me. "Oh, David," she whispered. Her voice started breaking. "We'll get through this together."

But even as I held her, I couldn't shake the fear that gripped me. The road ahead would be fraught with challenges, and I had to face the haunting shadows of my past again. I was ready to fight, but I couldn't help but wonder if I would emerge victorious or if I was already running out of time.

That night, as we settled into bed, I looked over at Mia's crib where she slept peacefully. The weight of my diagnosis settled heavily in my chest. The thought of leaving her without a father sent a chill down my spine. I couldn't let Hannah raise Mia alone. I had to fight—not just for myself but for them.

As the shadows of the night closed in, I realized that I was standing at a crossroads. I could either continue down the path of self-destruction or muster the strength to confront my demons.

With my family's love as my anchor, I knew I had to choose the lat-
ter. The journey ahead would be difficult, but for Mia and Hannah,
I would do whatever it took to reclaim my life. As I laid there, the
darkness of uncertainty pressed against me, but I felt a flicker of hope
igniting within. Maybe, just maybe, I could overcome this battle and
emerge stronger on the other side.

18

A NEW RESOLVE

The days that followed my doctor's visit felt like a whirlwind. I was caught in a storm of emotions—fear, shame, and a flicker of hope. Each morning, I would wake up beside Hannah and watch as she tended to our baby Mia with gentle care. Her love radiated through our small home and reminded me of everything I was fighting for, but also of the stakes I faced.

I had promised Hannah I would stop drinking, but the pull of old habits was strong. I found myself wrestling with the urge to pour a drink after a long day to escape the reality of my diagnosis. But every time I considered it, I thought of Mia's small face. Her innocent gaze looking up at me renewed my determination to fight.

One evening, as I sat on the porch watching the sunset, I felt a sense of clarity wash over me. It was time to confront my demons head-on. I needed help and I had to be honest with myself—and with Hannah.

That night, after putting Mia to bed, I turned to Hannah as we settled into the living room. "Can we talk?" I began as my heart pounded with the weight of my confession.

"Of course," she replied while setting her book aside. Her expression was attentive.

"I've been thinking about what the doctor said," I admitted. "I want to go back to POSSE. I need to address this drinking problem seriously."

Hannah's eyes lit up with relief. She reached for my hand. "I'm so proud of you for recognizing that," she said while squeezing my fingers. "It's a big step and I'm here for you every step of the way."

"I want to be better—for you and for Mia," I said while feeling the weight of my responsibility settle over me. "But I know it won't be easy."

"Nothing worth having ever is," she replied. Her voice filled with conviction. "We're in this together."

With her support, I began to prepare for my return to the POSSE group. The last time I had attended, I had found camaraderie and understanding among fellow officers. It was a safe space to share my struggles. The first meeting back was daunting; I sat in a circle with familiar faces. My heart raced as I prepared to share my story. But as I listened to others recount their struggles, I realized I wasn't alone. Their vulnerability inspired me. When it was my turn to speak, I finally felt the weight of my secrets lift.

"I've been hiding my drinking for years," I admitted. My voice was trembling. "I thought I could manage it, but it's taken a toll on my health, my family... on everything I care about."

The group listened intently while nodding in understanding. When I finished, a wave of relief washed over me. I was no longer alone in my fight.

As the weeks went by, I committed myself to the program. I attended meetings regularly and learned healthier coping mechanisms. Each session brought me closer to understanding the roots of my addiction. I found solace in the shared experiences of others. With each passing day, I felt stronger.

At home, I noticed a shift in my relationship with Hannah. We communicated more openly and I made a conscious effort to be present. We spent evenings together playing with Mia, laughing, and creating memories that reminded me of what I had almost lost.

One afternoon, we took Mia for a stroll in her stroller at the park. The sun was shining brightly and the laughter of children filled the air. Watching Hannah gently interact with Mia—talking to her, acknowledging the squirrels, and pointing out the flowers—filled me with an overwhelming sense of gratitude. This was what I was fighting for—a chance to be a good father and a good husband.

But as the sun began to set, I felt a familiar twinge in my side. I brushed it off and convinced myself that it was just a lingering reminder of my health issues. However, the worry crept back in. A shadow lurked at the edges of my mind.

Later that night, as we tucked Mia into her crib, I felt a sense of peace wash over me. I had made it through another day without drinking and I was proud of the progress I had made. But as I laid in bed beside Hannah, sleep eluded me. The pain in my side had returned. It was sharper this time and I couldn't shake the feeling that something was wrong.

"I can't keep this from her," I thought as the weight of my fear pressed down on me.

As I turned to Hannah, her gentle breathing calmed me. I knew I had to be honest with her about everything: not just my drinking, but any pain I was experiencing. I didn't want to hide anymore.

"Hey, Hannah?" I whispered. My voice broke the stillness of the night.

"Hmm?" she murmured sleepily while turning to face me.

"I want to tell you something," I began while feeling the tension in my chest tighten. "I've been feeling pain in my side again. I think I need to see the doctor again."

She opened her eyes as concern flooded her features. "Why didn't you tell me sooner? You need to take care of yourself."

"I will," I promised. The fear in her eyes was hard to bear. "I just... I didn't want to worry you."

"You're not a burden, David. We're in this together, remember?"

In that moment, I knew I couldn't protect her from my struggles. I had to be honest, not just about my drinking but about my health as well. "I promise I'll make an appointment," I said while holding her hand tightly.

As I drifted off to sleep, the pain lingered in my side. It was a reminder that I had battles ahead. Despite, I felt a renewed sense of determination to face whatever came next. I had a family that needed me and I was ready to fight for them.

However, as I closed my eyes, a nagging thought crept into my mind: What if the fight was harder than I anticipated? The shadows of uncertainty loomed large. As I sank into a restless sleep, I couldn't shake the feeling that the real battle was only just beginning.

19

SHADOWS OF DECEPTION

Returning to work after my time away felt like stepping back into a whirlwind. The familiar chaos of the precinct enveloped me. I was grateful for the routine, even if it was a reminder of the battles I still faced. Each day brought me closer to feeling like myself again, but the challenges of my past lingered, especially the call of alcohol that I had fought so hard to resist.

One day, while working undercover, I found myself in the thick of an operation aimed at dismantling a local drug ring. For months, we had been gathering intel and infiltrating their operations. I was determined to see it through. My partner, Officer Brown and I were deep in the heart of the investigation. The pressure was palpable.

As we made our way through a dimly lit warehouse, I felt a familiar twinge in my side. It was sharper this time. I brushed it off to focus on the task at hand. The adrenaline coursed through me as we approached our target—a known dealer who had eluded capture for far too long.

Suddenly, the air thickened with tension, and before I knew it, a pursuit ensued. The dealer bolted and I instinctively took off after him. As I sprinted, the pain in my side flared up. This was a brutal reminder of my health struggles. I stumbled. My body betrayed me in a moment where I needed to be at my best.

"Get him, Nigeria!" Brown shouted. His voice echoed behind me.

I pushed through the pain, but it was no use. Just then, I saw Brown take off like a shot to close the distance between himself and the suspect. With a burst of energy, he tackled the dealer to the ground and brought him down with a thud that echoed through the warehouse.

"Gotcha!" Brown exclaimed while securing the cuffed suspect. He looked back at me with a grin plastered on his face. "What happened, Nigeria? You not getting old on me, are you?"

I laughed slightly while trying to shake off the embarrassment and switch the subject. "Just a little rusty, that's all," I replied. I felt the weight of my hidden struggles pressing down on me.

For months, we had been working on this case and I couldn't afford any weaknesses. But as we wrapped up the scene, I felt the familiar urge to drink creep in again. The undercover work often involved blending in with the very people we were trying to take down. I had already found myself in situations where I had to force a drink into my hand to maintain my cover—a dangerous game.

"Hey, let's grab a drink after this," Brown suggested while slapping me on the back. "You've earned it."

I hesitated as the conflict raged inside me. My doctor had made it clear that I needed to stop drinking for my health, but in the world of undercover work, loyalty to the team often meant playing the part—even if it meant ignoring the advice of the very people trying to help me.

"Sure, sounds good," I replied while masking my inner turmoil. Torn between my job and my health, I found myself choosing my cover over my well-being. It was a slippery slope and I knew I was dancing with danger. However, the thrill of the job and the camaraderie of my partner pulled me in.

The night wore on, and as we returned to the precinct, I felt the tension in my shoulders ease slightly. We had successfully apprehended the dealer and the excitement of the chase lingered in the air.

But as Brown and I headed to a local bar to celebrate, I felt the familiar pull of temptation. The atmosphere was lively as the laughter of colleagues mingled with the clink of glasses. I ordered a drink. I told myself it was just one—just to fit in and celebrate our success.

As I took a sip, I felt a rush of conflicting emotions. The alcohol was a fleeting escape, but I knew it was a dangerous game. I could feel the shadows of my past creeping back in, but a part of me welcomed the numbing sensation. It was a temporary relief.

Suddenly, my phone buzzed in my pocket. It was a message from Hannah: "Just checking in. Love you."

I paused and stared at the screen. Guilt washed over me. I couldn't let her down again. I had promised to fight for my family, and here I was, slipping back into old habits.

Just as I was about to set the drink aside, an urgent call came through the radio. "All units, we have a situation developing at the warehouse! Officers needed immediately!"

My heart raced as adrenaline surged through me. I glanced at Brown, who was already on his feet, ready to respond. "Looks like we've got work to do," he said. His eyes gleamed with excitement.

We rushed out. The thrill of the chase ignited a fire in my belly. As we approached the warehouse, I felt the weight of the moment. This was my purpose. The darkness of my struggles faded into the background and were replaced by the adrenaline of the job.

As we arrived on the scene, chaos erupted. A shootout had begun and I could feel the urgency in the air. My instincts kicked in. I pushed through the crowd of officers and focused on the task ahead.

"Stay close!" Brown shouted as we maneuvered through the warehouse. We were dodging bullets and taking cover. The rush of action was intoxicating. It was pulling me deeper into the chaos.

In the midst of it all, the pain in my side flared up again. It was sharper and more insistent. I gritted my teeth and tried to ignore it. I focused solely on the task at hand. This was my chance to prove myself and show my loyalty to the team.

As we cornered the suspects, the tension reached a boiling point. Shots rang out. I moved instinctively while adrenaline masked the pain. Unfortunately, as I took a step forward, I felt a surge of agony that brought me to my knees.

"Officer Nigeria!" Brown shouted while rushing to my side as I collapsed. "What's wrong?"

The world around me spun and I could see the concern etched on Brown's face. "I'm fine," I gasped, but the truth was undeniable—I was in trouble.

As the chaos continued around us, I realized that I was facing a battle far greater than I had anticipated. In that moment, the thrill of the chase faded as the reality of my situation settled in. I was fighting, not just for my job, but for my life.

As I laid there, the shadows of my past closed in. I knew I had to confront the darkness once and for all.

Then, everything went black.

20

A FIGHT FOR LIFE

I woke up to an antiseptic smell that invaded my senses. A dim light above me flickered. I blinked against the brightness as confusion clouded my mind. Where was I?

Slowly, I turned my head and the scene around me came into focus. I was in a hospital room. The steady beep of a monitor echoed in the silence. Panic surged through me as I attempted to sit up, but a wave of dizziness washed over me. I collapsed back onto the pillow.

"Easy there, Nigeria," a familiar voice said. I turned and saw Officer Brown standing at the foot of the bed with concern etched across his face. "You gave us a scare."

"What happened?" I croaked. My throat was dry and scratchy.

"You went down during the shootout." he said. His expression was solemn. "You're in the hospital now."

Just then, the door opened, and Hannah rushed in. Her eyes were wide with worry. "David!" she exclaimed while rushing to my side.

Seeing her brought a rush of relief, but also a wave of guilt. "Hannah, I... I didn't mean for this to happen," I managed as my voice trembled.

Tears filled her eyes as she grasped my hand. "Don't you dare apologize. We were so scared. You scared us all."

I looked around the room and noticed my colleagues—some of whom had been by my side during the operation—standing quietly in the background. Their expressions were a mixture of relief and concern. A palpable tension hung in the air.

"What's going on?" I asked. My heart raced as I tried to piece together the fragments of my memory.

"You were unconscious for a while," Brown chimed in. "They had to stabilize you. You were bleeding internally, Nigeria. They had to do surgery."

Surgery? The word hung in the air like a weight. Panic rose within me and I squeezed Hannah's hand tighter. "Am I going to be okay?"

The room fell silent and I could see the worry in everyone's eyes, including Hannah's. "The doctors are doing everything they can," she said softly while trying to reassure me, but that did not quell my fear.

Just then, I noticed a small figure in the corner of the room—Mia, my baby girl, nestled in her carrier. Her tiny body was wrapped in a soft blanket. My heart ached at the sight of her. She was innocent and unaware of the turmoil surrounding her.

"I'm here, baby," I whispered while trying to reach out to her. However, my body felt so weak and so fragile.

Hannah turned to Brown as her voice thickened with emotion. "I haven't told him yet..." she began. Her eyes glistened with unshed tears. "About his health... about the drinking."

Brown nodded as understanding dawned in his gaze. "You should, Hannah. He needs to know what he's up against."

Hannah took a deep breath. Her gaze was steady as she turned back to me. "David, there's something I need to tell you. The doctor... he said the drinking has really taken a toll on your liver. This isn't just a one-time thing; it's serious."

I felt the weight of her words settle over me like a shroud. The truth I had tried to escape from was crashing down around me. "I thought I could manage it," I whispered as the guilt flooded in. "I didn't want to let you down."

"You didn't let us down," she said. Her voice was fierce. "You're fighting for your life right now. We're all here for you and we're going to get through this together."

Tears streamed down my cheeks as I took in her words. I was not just fighting for myself; I was fighting for my family. The thought of leaving them was unbearable. How could I miss seeing Mia grow up?

"Please, just promise me you'll try," Hannah urged while squeezing my hand. "For Mia. For us."

With every ounce of strength I had, I nodded. Despite, doubt swirled in my mind. Would I make it? Could I overcome this?

As the hours dragged on, I drifted in and out of consciousness. The pain in my side throbbed with an intensity that made it hard to focus. Each time I opened my eyes, I was met with the worried faces of my colleagues, the love of my wife, and the innocent gaze of my daughter.

I could hear snippets of conversations around me. Brown was relaying stories of our operations in an attempt to lighten the mood. Laughter mingled with the tension, but I could feel the undercurrent of fear.

"I'll get you back on the streets, Nigeria," Brown joked lightly. However, I sensed the seriousness behind his words. "You're not getting out of this that easily."

The reality was, I was in a fight for my life. This was one I couldn't afford to lose. As I laid there, the darkness crept in. I realized that this was my moment to change—to confront my demons and to choose my family over my past.

With a deep breath, I focused on Hannah, on Mia, and the life I wanted to fight for. I would face whatever came next, not just for myself, but for them. I wouldn't let the shadows of my past dictate my future.

As the night wore on, I felt the weight of my choices settling in. I was ready to fight and reclaim my life. However, as the uncertainty loomed over me, I couldn't help but wonder if I had the strength to see it through.

In that moment, I made a silent vow: I would not go quietly into the night. I would rise up and I fight—for my family, for my future, and for the chance to truly live.

21

THE FIGHT WITHIN

The hospital room was a blur of sterile white walls and the rhythmic beeping of machines. Each sound echoed in my mind. They were a reminder of the battle I was waging, not just against the physical pain in my side, but against the demons I had allowed to take root in my life.

As I laid there, the weight of my diagnosis pressed heavily on my chest. I could hear the muffled sounds of conversations outside my room, but inside, it felt like I was in a bubble. I felt isolated from the world. The faces of my colleagues, my wife, and my baby girl were the only anchors I had.

Days blended together. Each one was a test of my resolve. The doctors came and went. Their expressions were serious, yet hopeful. They reminded me that there was a path forward if I was willing to embrace it. The journey ahead was daunting; it was filled with the uncertainty of my health and the shadows of my past that loomed ever closer.

One afternoon, as I tried to sit up, I felt a wave of nausea crash over me. I was still weak from the surgery. The pain in my side was a constant reminder of how close I had come to losing everything.

Just then, the door creaked open and Hannah walked in with a smile breaking through her worry.

"Hey, you," she said softly with her eyes lighting up as she approached my bedside. "How are you feeling today?"

I managed a weak smile, but the truth was, I felt lost. "Like I've been hit by a truck," I admitted in a hoarse voice.

She chuckled gently but her concern was palpable. "You've been through a lot. It's going to take time."

"I know," I replied as my gaze drifted to Mia. She was nestled in her carrier beside Hannah. The sight of her brought a rush of love and pain. "I just want to be there for both of you. I don't want to let you down again."

"You're not going to let us down," Hannah said firmly. Her expression was resolute. "You're fighting for your life and that's what matters right now. We're in this together."

Her words wrapped around me like a lifeline, but the fear still gnawed at the edges of my mind. "What if I can't do this?" I whispered as vulnerability crept into my voice.

"You can," she insisted while squeezing my hand. "You have to believe that. Remember what we talked about? Facing your demons, taking it one step at a time?"

I nodded but doubt still lingered. "It's just... the drinking. I thought I could control it, but now I feel like I'm fighting against my own body."

Hannah's eyes softened. "You're stronger than you think. You've already taken the first steps by being honest with me and seeking help. That's not easy."

Just then, Brown popped his head in. His expression was a mixture of seriousness and camaraderie. "Hey, Nigeria! I just wanted to check in on you. We are all worried about you!"

"Yeah, well, I didn't plan on being the center of attention," I replied, trying to inject some humor, though it fell flat.

"Don't worry; we're all just glad you're still with us," he said while pulling up a chair. "The team's been talking and we're ready to back you up. You need anything, you let us know."

"Thanks, Brown," I said while feeling a swell of gratitude for my partner's support. "I appreciate it."

As we talked, I felt a sense of normalcy begin to return,. This was a reminder of the life I was fighting to reclaim. But as the conversation continued, the reality of my situation crept back in.

"Have you thought about what comes next?" Brown asked. His tone became serious. "The doctor mentioned you'll need a plan for recovery."

"I have," I admitted as the weight of my choices settled back in. "I want to focus on my health but I also need to figure out how to do this job without falling back into old habits."

"Just remember, you're not alone in this," Brown said with a steady gaze. "And if you ever need to talk, I'm here."

As the hours passed, I felt a shift within myself. The pain was still there, but so was a burgeoning resolve. I had a choice to make—not just about my health, but about the kind of father and husband I wanted to be.

Later that evening, as the sun set outside my hospital window and casted warm hues across the room, I took a moment to reflect on everything that had happened. I was scared, yes, but I was also determined. I wouldn't let my past define me any longer.

As Hannah rocked Mia in her arms, I made a silent vow. I would fight for my health, for my family, and for the chance to show them the man I could become. It wouldn't be easy, but I was ready to face whatever came next.

As I began to feel that flicker of hope ignite within me, the pain in my side surged again. It was more intense this time. I winced. I tried to suppress a gasp, but the discomfort was undeniable.

"Are you okay?" Hannah asked with her brow furrowing in concern.

"Yeah, just... a little pain," I lied, but I could see the worry etched in her features.

And then, as if the universe had decided to remind me of my fragility, the hospital room door swung open. The doctor walked in with a serious expression. "Officer Nigeria, we need to discuss your recovery plan and some concerning test results."

A sense of dread washed over me as I caught Hannah's eye. The flicker of hope that had been building inside me dimmed. It was replaced by a wave of anxiety. Would I be able to fight through this? What new challenges awaited me?

As I braced myself for whatever news was coming, I felt the weight of my journey ahead settle over me. The battle for my life was far from over. I knew I had to dig deep to find the strength I needed to face the uncertainty that laid ahead.

22

STEPS TOWARD RECOVERY

The days in the hospital blurred together, but amidst the uncertainty, I found a renewed sense of purpose. The doctor's words echoed in my mind: I had to confront, not only my physical health, but the emotional scars that had driven me to drink in the first place. The doctor informed me that I had Hepatic Cirrhosis.

After the initial shock of my diagnosis, I had agreed to a recovery plan that included therapy. I knew I needed to delve into the depths of my struggles. I had to understand the roots of my addiction if I was ever going to break free from its grip.

Once I was stable enough to leave my hospital bed, I began attending therapy sessions in the hospital and at a nearby outpatient program. The first session was daunting. I sat in a small, sunlit room, surrounded by soft chairs and a sense of unease. A therapist named Dr. Patel sat across from me. She had a calm demeanor while inviting me to share my story.

"Tell me about what brought you here," she prompted gently. Her voice was soothing.

I hesitated with the weight of my experiences heavy on my heart. "I've been struggling with alcohol for years," I admitted while feeling the vulnerability wash over me. "I thought I could control it, but it spiraled out of control. I didn't realize how much it was affecting my health, my family... everything."

Dr. Patel nodded with an understanding expression. "Acknowledging that is a significant first step. It takes a lot of courage to confront these issues. How do you feel about your drinking now?"

"I feel ashamed," I said. My voice cracked. "I've let my family down. They've been my support and I've put them through so much."

"Shame can be a heavy burden to carry," she replied. "But it's important to remember that recovery is a journey. It's about learning and growing, not just about stopping the behavior."

As our sessions continued, I began to peel back the layers of my past. I explored the pressures of my job, the expectations I had placed on myself, and the moments when I had turned to alcohol as a coping mechanism. Each session was a cathartic release and a chance to confront the emotions I had buried for too long.

Meanwhile, at home, Hannah was my rock. She attended family therapy sessions alongside me with an eagerness to understand my struggles. She wanted to learn how she could support me better. Watching her dedication filled me with gratitude and a renewed sense of responsibility.

One evening, after a particularly intense session, I returned home feeling emotionally drained. I found Hannah in the kitchen preparing dinner. Her movements were fluid and graceful. Mia was in her high chair, giggling, as she played with her toys.

"Hey, how did it go?" Hannah asked with a smile brightening the room.

"It was tough," I admitted while dropping into a chair at the kitchen table. "But I think it's helping. I'm starting to understand what drives me to drink."

"I'm proud of you for facing it head-on," she said while setting down the spatula and coming over to kiss my forehead. "You're doing the hard work, and it's going to pay off."

As days turned into weeks, I began to notice changes within myself. I felt lighter, as if the weight of my past was slowly lifting. I learned coping strategies to deal with stress and I embraced healthier outlets, like exercise and journaling. Each time I chose a healthier path over alcohol, I felt a small victory.

But the road wasn't without its bumps. There were days when the cravings surged. The urge to drink threatened to pull me under. On those days, I would lean on Hannah or call Brown. I had to remind myself of the support I had around me.

One afternoon, during a session focused on triggers, I shared a moment from the previous week that had shaken me. "I was at the store and I passed the liquor aisle. My heart raced and I felt this overwhelming pull to grab a bottle. It was like I was being drawn back into the darkness."

Dr. Patel nodded and encouraged me to explore those feelings. "What did you do in that moment?"

"I walked away," I said with pride swelling in my chest. "I reminded myself of Mia and Hannah. I couldn't let them down again."

"Exactly," she said as her eyes shined with approval. "Every time you choose to walk away, you're taking back your power. Recovery is about those small victories."

As the weeks continued to pass, I gradually transitioned back to work. That prospect was daunting. I was determined to prove to myself that I could balance my responsibilities while prioritizing my health.

Returning to the precinct felt surreal. My colleagues welcomed me back with open arms, and Brown, of course, was making light of the situation to ease my nerves. "Glad to see you back, old man," he joked while clapping me on the shoulder. "Just don't go passing out on us again!"

I laughed, but inside, I felt the weight of my journey. I had to navigate this new life: one where I could no longer rely on alcohol to cope.

As I settled back into the routine, I found myself facing a new challenge. The pressure of the job, combined with the expectations I had placed on myself, sometimes felt overwhelming. There were moments when I felt the urge to slip back into the familiar comfort of a drink, but I would pause, take a breath, and remind myself of everything I had to lose.

One late evening, as we wrapped up a case, I found myself in a tense situation that tested my resolve. We were on the trail of a suspect involved in a drug deal and the stakes were high. As we cornered the suspect, adrenaline surged through me. I felt the familiar thrill of the chase.

As the situation escalated, the pain in my side flared up again. I gritted my teeth and pushed through the discomfort. I was determined to stay focused. I couldn't let my health interfere with my job—this was my chance to prove that I could do this, that I could be the officer I had always aspired to be.

As the confrontation unfolded, I felt the tension in the air. It was a reminder that I was still in a fight—not just against external threats, but against the internal struggles that had haunted me for so long.

With every choice I made, I was building a new future: one where I could stand tall for my family and for myself. As I took a deep breath, I knew that I was ready to face whatever challenges laid ahead. I was fighting for my life and for the love that awaited me at home.

23

REFLECTIONS

As I settled into the rhythmic hum of the night, I found myself lying awake with the darkness wrapping around me like a familiar blanket. The quiet of the house was both comforting and unsettling. It was during these solitary moments that the gravity of my journey weighed most heavily upon me. It urged me to reflect on how far I had come—and how much further I still had to go.

The events of the past few months played out in my mind like a movie reel. Each frame was a vivid reminder of the battles I had fought. I thought back to my time in the hospital and the uncertainty that gripped me as I faced my diagnosis. The fear of not being there for Hannah and Mia was a heavy burden. It drove me to confront my demons head-on.

I could still hear Hannah's voice that filled with concern and love as she urged me to fight for my health. It was a reminder of the stakes involved in my recovery. I wasn't just battling addiction; I was fighting for my family and the future I wanted to build. The thought of leaving them without a father and letting them down again sent a shiver down my spine.

Then, there were the therapy sessions with Dr. Patel. I had approached those meetings with trepidation, but they had become a source of strength. Each discussion peeled back layers of my past and exposed the roots of my addiction. I had learned to confront my feelings rather than bury them. I also learned to seek help instead of hide in shame. This journey had been about more than stopping the drinking—it was about understanding the man I had become and the man I wanted to be.

The memories of my colleagues flooded my thoughts: Brown's unwavering support, the camaraderie that had pulled me through challenging times, and the moments of laughter amidst the chaos. I realized that being a part of a team wasn't just about sharing the successes; it was also about leaning on each other during the struggles. I had often felt the weight of my job pressing down on me, but I was learning that vulnerability was not a sign of weakness; it was a bridge that connected me to others.

Mia's laughter echoed in my mind: a sound that filled my heart with warmth and purpose. Each time I held her, I felt a renewed sense of responsibility. I wanted to be the father who was present and guided her through life with love and strength. The thought of her growing up without my guidance fueled my determination to stay on the path of recovery.

But the reflections weren't always easy. The shadows of my past still lingered and whispered doubts into my mind. What if I stumbled? What if I faltered and fell back into old habits? Each time I thought of taking a drink, I reminded myself of the promise I made—not just to Hannah and Mia, but to myself. I had to face the discomfort head-on. I knew that the road to recovery was filled with ups and downs.

I took a deep breath while feeling the weight of my journey settle on my shoulders. I had come a long way, but I knew I couldn't let my guard down. I had to remain vigilant. It was critical for me to be conscious of the choices I made each day.

As I laid there, I realized that my reflections were, not just about the battles I had fought, but also about the victories I had achieved. I was learning to live in the moment and embrace each day as an opportunity for growth. I was discovering the beauty of connection—first with Hannah, then with Mia, and finally with myself.

The journey ahead was still uncertain, but I felt a flicker of determination igniting within me. I would face the challenges, confront the shadows, and continue to fight for the life I wanted. I had the power to rewrite my story and emerge from the darkness stronger than before.

With that thought, I closed my eyes and allowed the quiet of the night to wash over me. I was ready for whatever came next with a determination to embrace each moment with courage, love, and the unwavering belief that I could overcome anything.

As I drifted into a peaceful sleep, I felt the weight of my past begin to lift. It was replaced by the promise of a brighter future: one filled with hope and resilience.

24

THE EDGE OF DARKNESS

Returning to work felt both exhilarating and terrifying. The precinct buzzed with activity; the familiar sounds of ringing phones and hurried footsteps grounded me in a reality I had fought so hard to reclaim. Yet, beneath the surface, the anxieties of my past lingered like a shadow. It reminded me of the precarious balance I was trying to maintain.

As I settled into my desk, I glanced around at my colleagues who were each engrossed in their tasks. Brown caught my eye from across the room and gave me a nod with a reassuring smile on his face. We had been through a lot together and I knew he had my back. But the weight of my recovery felt heavier in this environment. The pressure to perform was palpable.

Later that day, I found myself in a briefing about an ongoing investigation into a local drug ring. The adrenaline surged through me as we went over the details. The excitement of the job ignited a fire within. However, alongside that excitement was a nagging fear—a whisper reminding me of my struggles with alcohol.

"Alright, team, we need to stay focused," the lieutenant said as if he broke into my thoughts. "This operation is crucial and we need everyone at their best."

I nodded, but the tension in my chest tightened. I was determined to show my commitment and prove that I could be the officer my family and team needed. As the day wore on, the stress mounted. I felt the old urges rising within me.

After a long shift filled with high-pressure situations, I clocked out. The weight of the day settled heavily on my shoulders. I knew I had to go home to Hannah and Mia, but the thought of facing the evening without a drink was daunting. Just one drink to take the edge off, I thought. It would help me unwind.

Against my better judgment, I found myself stopping at a bar on the way home. The dim lighting and the familiar atmosphere pulled me in. As I sat at the bar, I felt a wave of nostalgia wash over me. The bartender greeted me like an old friend. I ordered a drink. Feeling the warmth of the alcohol settle into my veins like a comforting embrace.

As I took my first sip, the world around me faded and the worries of the day slipped away. I told myself it was just one drink: a moment of weakness that wouldn't define me. But deep down, I felt the familiar tug of addiction beckoning and whispering promises of relief that I knew were false.

After finishing my drink, I felt a momentary sense of calm, but it was quickly replaced by guilt. I had promised Hannah I would stop. I had vowed to fight for my family, yet here I was, slipping back into the very habits I had fought so hard to escape.

As I left the bar, the effects of the alcohol began to cloud my judgment. The streets blurred before me and I felt the weight of my choices bearing down. I was caught in a dangerous cycle: torn between the desire to escape and the responsibility I had to my family.

Then, in a moment of reckless decision, I climbed into my car. The engine roared to life and I felt a rush of adrenaline mixed with dread. I told myself I could handle it. I'd be fine. However, as I pulled onto the road, the combination of alcohol and adrenaline clouded my senses.

Halfway home, everything went dark.

I awoke to the sound of sirens and the bright lights of a police cruiser illuminating the night. Confusion enveloped me as I realized the front end of my car was crumpled against a streetlight. Panic surged through me and I fumbled for my phone. My heart raced as the reality of the situation set in.

"Officer Nigeria!" a voice called out. I looked up to see the officer approaching. His expression was a mixture of concern and disappointment. "What the hell happened?"

"I... I don't know," I stammered with my voice shaking. "I was just driving home."

"Do you even realize what you've done?" he said in a sharp tone. "You're intoxicated, Nigeria. This is serious."

The weight of his words crashed down on me and I felt the heat of shame wash over me. I had let my family down again. As the officers approached, I could see the flash of the handcuffs. The reality of my situation closed in.

"Please," I pleaded with desperation seeping into my voice. "I can explain. This isn't who I am."

However, the officers were already pulling me from the car. The weight of my choices settled over me like a shroud. I could feel the tears prick at my eyes as the realization of what I had done crashed over me like a wave. I had fought so hard to reclaim my life; however, I let it slip through my fingers in an instant.

As I was placed in the back of the cruiser, I could see the officer's disappointed gaze. The hurt was reflected in his eyes. "You better get your act together, Nigeria. This isn't just about you anymore," he said. His voice was steady but laced with concern.

I hung my head as the gravity of my situation crashed down like a tidal wave. I was facing, not just arrest, but the potential loss of everything I had fought for—my family, my job, my future.

As I sat in the back of the cruiser, I felt the tears fall freely. I had let the darkness pull me back in and now I was paying the price. The thought of Hannah and Mia waiting for me at home crushed me.

"Please, God," I whispered to the empty night, "give me the strength to fight this."

In that moment of despair, I felt a flicker of determination ignite once more. I would not let this define me. No matter how hard the road ahead would be, I would rise from this.

As the cruiser pulled away, I knew the real battle was just beginning.

***

TO BE CONTINUED

Self-Help Guide to Recovering from Addiction

Recovering from addiction is a journey that requires self-discovery, planning, and execution. This guide will help you navigate the process by identifying your motivations, creating a personalized recovery plan, and executing steps toward a healthier life.

Step 1: Discover Your Why

Understanding the reasons behind your desire to overcome addiction is crucial. Reflect on the following questions:

1. What does addiction take away from you?

- Think about relationships, health, career, and happiness.

2. What do you want to gain?

- Consider aspirations, wellness, freedom, and peace of mind.

3. Who else is affected by your addiction?

- Reflect on loved ones, friends, and colleagues, and how they feel about your situation.

4. What are your core values?

- Identify what matters most to you (e.g., family, integrity, health) and how addiction conflicts with those values.

5. Visualize your future.

- Picture a life free from addiction. What does it look like? How do you feel?

Step 2: Create Your How

Once you've identified your motivation, develop a structured plan for recovery. Consider the following components:

1. Set Clear Goals:
   - Establish short-term and long-term goals. Make them SMART (Specific, Measurable, Achievable, Relevant, Time-bound).

2. Identify Triggers:
   - Recognize situations, people, or emotions that lead to cravings. Develop strategies to cope with or avoid these triggers.

3. Build a Support System:
   - Surround yourself with positive influences. This can include friends, family, support groups, or therapists.

4. Develop Healthy Coping Mechanisms:
   - Identify activities that promote well-being, such as exercise, meditation, hobbies, or volunteering.

5. Educate Yourself:
   - Learn about addiction and recovery. Understanding the science behind addiction can empower you.

6. Establish a Routine:
   - Create a daily schedule that incorporates healthy habits, self-care, and time for reflection.

Step 3: Execute

With your plan in place, it's time to take action. Here are steps for effective execution:

1. Start Small:

- Begin with manageable steps. Celebrate small victories to build momentum.

2. Stay Accountable:

- Share your goals with someone you trust. Regular check-ins can help you stay on track.

3. Reflect and Adjust:

- Regularly assess your progress. If something isn't working, be willing to adjust your approach.

4. Practice Self-Compassion:

- Understand that setbacks may occur. Don't be too hard on yourself; treat yourself with kindness and learn from challenges.

5. Seek Professional Help:

- Consider therapy or counseling. Professionals can provide support and strategies tailored to your needs.

6. Engage in Healthy Activities:

Fill your time with positive experiences that reinforce your commitment to recovery.

7. Keep a Journal:

Document your feelings, progress, and challenges. This can provide insights and help you stay focused.

Conclusion

Recovering from addiction is a personal journey that requires dedication, self-awareness, and a solid plan. By discovering your "why," creating a comprehensive "how," and executing your plan with determination, you can reclaim your life and build a brighter, healthier future. Remember, it's a process—be patient with yourself and celebrate your progress along the way.

POSSE

POLICE OFFICER SOBRIETY SUPPORT ENBLOC
"Helping to Save the Lives Who Protect Ours"

ABOUT US

The Police Officer Sobriety Support Enbloc program is a nonprofit organization dedicated to providing support, resources, and intervention for police officers who struggle with substance abuse. The program's goal is to promote the safety and well-being of police officers throughout the nation by preventing and addressing substance abuse among law enforcement personnel. The program provides a confidential, supportive, and non-punitive environment for officers to seek help and treatment for substance abuse. The program aims to reduce the negative impact of substance abuse on individual officers, their families, and the communities they serve.

SOLUTION ACTIVITIES

Curriculum and Activities

The curriculum and activities of the Police Officer Sobriety Intervention program are designed to address the unique needs and challenges faced by police officers in relation to substance abuse. Some of the key components of the program include:

- **Stress management**: The program provides education and resources on stress management techniques, as stress is often a contributing factor to substance abuse among police officers.

- **Nutrition and exercise**: The program emphasize the importance of proper nutrition and exercise for physical and mental health, and provides resources and support for officers looking to adopt healthier habits.

- **Support and accountability**: The program provide support and accountability resources, including peer support groups and regular check-ins with program staff, to help officers stay on track with their sobriety goals.

- **Intervention and referral**: The program provide training and resources on identifying and intervening with officers who may be struggling with substance abuse, as well as referral resources for officers who need more intensive treatment.

SOLUTION TO THE CHALLENGE OF POLICE DRUG AND ALCOHOL ABUSE

The Purpose of Our Help

The purpose in helping to restore the lives of those who protect ours is to assist in the restoration and rehabilitation of police officers who are struggling with drug and alcohol abuse. As a program specifically designed to provide the necessary support, resources, and interventions to help police officers overcome addiction and rebuild their lives, the objective will be by supporting Officer(s) well-being. POSSE understands the unique challenges and stressors faced by law enforcement personnel, and therefore, aim to provide a safe and confidential environment where officers can seek help without fear of judgment or repercussions. By addressing their substance abuse issues, the program will help restore their physical and mental health and enhance their job performance. This will contribute to their overall wellbeing.

POSSE SEEKS YOUR SUPPORT, VOLUNTEER HELP, AND CONTRIBUTIONS

Community Support

Engaging with the community will be a cornerstone of our fundraising efforts. POSSE will organize fundraising campaigns that directly involve community members, fostering a sense of ownership and pride in supporting our cause. Through various channels, such as social media, local events, and community partnerships, we will actively sock donations, both monetary and in-kind, from individuals and businesses within the community.

Another fine illustration to assert, we may launch a crowdfunding campaign that highlights the personal stories of police officers who have benefited from our program.

POSSE collaborates with local organizations, schools, and faith-based groups to organize fundraising events such as charity runs, benefit concerts, or community gatherings.

By emphasizing the positive impact community contributions have on the well-being of police officers and the overall safety of the community, we therefore inspire individuals and businesses to support our program financially.

Individual Donors

Aware of the importance of cultivating relationships with individuals who share the program's vision as well as understand the significance of supporting police officers' well-being.

CONFRONTING THE CHALLENGES OF DRUGS AND ALCOHOL ABUSE

Our Mission, Vision Statement, and Core Values:

Mission: To empower police officers in their journey to overcome drug and alcohol abuse, restore their lives, and promote a healthier and safer law enforcement community.

AS THE SOLUTION

POSSE provides access to a network of peer support: The program provides officers with access to a community of peers who have gone through similar experiences and can offer support and encouragement throughout the recovery process.

Ongoing support: The program offers ongoing support to participants, ensuring that they have access to the resources and guidance they need to maintain their sobriety and lead healthy, fulfilling lives.

GET IN TOUCH

Phone: (571) 662-5811, 1 (877) 79-POSSE or 1 (877) 797-6773
Mail: 10908 Courthouse Rd., Suite 102, Fredericksburg, VA 22408
Website: www.posse-usa.org

ABOUT THE AUTHOR
McCarthy Barnes Jr.

Early Life and Education

McCarthy Barnes Jr. was born and raised in Washington, D.C., on March 1, 1978. From a young age, he developed a keen interest in understanding society, which led him to study Criminal Justice. He is currently pursuing a Bachelor of Science in Psychology, further enhancing his foundation for a career dedicated to community service.

Career

McCarthy served as a law enforcement officer for over a decade, gaining invaluable experience in upholding the law and serving his community. This role instilled in him a deep understanding of the challenges faced by those in uniform and fueled his passion for supporting fellow officers.

As the Founder and Director of the Police Officer Sobriety Support Enbloc (POSSE), McCarthy brings a unique perspective to the organization. As a former police officer and a recovered alcoholic, his journey serves as a driving force behind POSSE. He witnessed the impact of substance abuse within law enforcement and recognized the need for specialized support tailored for officers struggling with addiction. He made it his mission to provide essential resources to his fellow officers.

Having experienced the struggles and triumphs of recovery, McCarthy is well-positioned to guide the program's direction. His personal journey offers a profound understanding of addiction and the specific challenges faced by law enforcement personnel. McCarthy's story serves as an inspiration and testament to recovery.

In addition to his work with POSSE, McCarthy transitioned to the pharmaceutical field, excelling in life coaching and management. His work reflects his commitment to personal and professional development, showcasing his ability to lead and inspire others.

Interests and Hobbies

Outside of his professional endeavors, McCarthy is an outdoor enthusiast. He enjoys fishing and camping—activities that allow him to connect with nature and unwind. These hobbies reflect his appreciation for a balanced lifestyle.

Conclusion

McCarthy Barnes Jr. is a dedicated professional in the pharmaceutical industry and a compassionate leader, committed to supporting law enforcement and promoting sobriety.

www.ingramcontent.com/pod-product-compliance
Lightning Source LLC
Chambersburg PA
CBHW060833120626
46557CB00001B/486